10 Steps to CREATING MEMORABLE CHARACTERS

FORMS, CHECKLISTS & EXERCISES
designed to help screen and fiction writers create
and develop exciting and unforgettable personalities

Sue Viders
Lucynda Storey
Cher Gorman
Becky Martinez

 lone eagle™

D1300675

10 Steps to Creating Memorable Characters

Forms, checklists, and exercises designed to help Screen and Fiction writers create and develop exciting and unforgettable personalities
Copyright © 2006 Viders, Storey, Gorman, Martinez

LONE EAGLE PUBLISHING COMPANY™
A Division of Watson-Guptill
770 Broadway
New York, NY 10003

ISBN-10: 1-58065-068-6
ISBN-13: 978-1-58065-068-7

Lone Eagle Publishing Company™ is a registered trademark.

Cover and book design by Carla Green
Edited by Steve Atinsky

Library of Congress Cataloging-in-Publication data:
    Viders, Sue.
10 steps to creating memorable characters : forms, checklists, and exercises designed to help screen and fiction writers create and develop exciting and unforgettable personalities / by Sue Viders... (et al.).
        p.   cm.
    ISBN 1-58065-068-6
    1. Fiction—Techniques. 2. Motion picture authorship. 3. Characters and characteristics in literature. I. Title.

    PN3383.C4 A14 2006
    808.3—dc22   2006045275

Coming soon...

DEVELOPING
A TRULY
ORIGINAL PLOT

BUILDING AN
UNFORGETTABLE SETTING

The Authors

Sue Viders	website	www.sueviders.com
	e-mail	sueviders@comcast.net
Lucynda Storey	website	www.lucyndastorey.com
	e-mail	cyn@realmsoflove.com
Cher Gorman	website	www.chergorman.com
	e-mail	cher@chergorman.com
Becky Martinez	website	www.rebeccagrace.com
	e-mail	goldbooks2@aol.com

Printed in the United States of America
10 9 8 7 6 5 4 3 2 1

DEDICATION

From **Sue Viders**:
This book could never have been written without my three critique co-authors. Once we embarked on this project, ideas flew fast and furious. Months of brain storming and editing brought the book together. Thanks, guys.

From **Lucynda Storey**:
To my family and beloved JR — I love you so much. Thanks for your encouragement and support. Thanks also to my critique partners for encouragement and insights, which make my writing better.

From **Cher Gorman**:
To the most wonderful critique partners on the planet: Becky, Lucynda, and Sue. You guys are the best. To Mike and Lilly for always being there.

From **Becky Martinez**:
Thanks to my sister Lillie and niece Shannan for their input, and a big thanks to my wonderful and helpful critique partners and co-authors.

Acknowledgment

From all of us:
Many thanks to the staff of the Le Peep's Restaurant for all their help and allowing us to sit and write for hours over our morning breakfast meetings.

CONTENTS

INTRODUCTION

What Comes First? x
Deciding on a GENRE. xii
Deciding on a Character's NAME. xvi
Whose Story Is It? POV xviii
Our Story — A Romantic Suspense Plot xx
How to Best Use This Book xxii

Step One   **PHYSICAL DESCRIPTION**

Overview 1
Age 2
Physique 4
Face 6
Distinguishing Characteristics. 8
Summary. 10

Step Two   **PROFESSION or OCCUPATION**

Overview 11
Work Ethic. 12
Profession or Occupation 14
Summary. 16

Step Three   **HISTORY**

Overview 17
Upbringing 18
Influences 20
Successes and Regrets 22
Defining Moments. 24
Time Line 26
Summary. 28

As you will note, there are several related topics in each section. Each topic has two pages: On the left side is text with explanations and several exercises, while on the right-hand page there is a worksheet with either a checklist of ideas or an appropriate form for you to consider.

Step Four **RELATIONSHIPS**

Overview 29
Family 30
Family's Background 32
Friends 34
Significant Other (S.O.) 36
Summary 38

Step Five **PERSONALITY**

Overview 39
Traits and Habits 40
Attitudes 42
Pet Peeves 46
Strengths and Weaknesses 48
Flaws and Fears 50
Secrets 52
Beliefs 54
Handling a Crisis 56
Skills and Talents 58
Soft Spot 60
Ambition(s) 62
Caring 64
Needs and Desires 66
Favorites 68
Self-Portrait 70
Summary 72

Step Six **BODY LANGUAGE and SPEECH**

Overview 73
Speech 76
Identifying Tags 78
Summary 80

Step Seven **WARDROBE and POSSESSIONS**

Overview 81
Wardrobe 82
Grooming 84
Vehicle(s) 86
Pet(s) 88
Most Prized Possession 90
Summary 92

Step Eight **ENVIRONMENT and DAILY LIVING**

Overview 93
Home 94
Office/Work Environment 96
Community 98
A Day in the Life of... 100
A Weekend in the Life of... 102
Summary 104

Sometimes you will know your character from the very beginning; other times your character will develop as the story progresses.

Step Nine   **THE CHARACTER DIAMOND**

Overview *105*
Crusade (What) *106*
Cause (Why) *110*
Complication (Problem) *114*
Change (End Result) *118*
Summary *122*

Step Ten   **PUTTING IT ALL TOGETHER**

Overview *123*
Kayla *124*
Quinn *126*
Emily *128*
Summary *130*

FINAL THOUGHTS

Overview *131*
Secondary Characters *132*
Off-Screen and Walk-On Characters *134*
Characters in Different Genres *136*
Final Thoughts *144*
Summary *148*

APPENDIX

Overview *149*
Worksheet for Main Character's Family *150*
Worksheet for Main Character's Friends *151*
Charts for Cast of Characters *152*
Checklist of Professions and Occupations *154*

INTRODUCTION

Great stories, books, plays, and movies need memorable characters as well as an interesting plot. This book, however, focuses only on how to write really great characters — people who come alive in the mind of the reader.

Before we begin our in-depth character analysis, we need to first discuss several writing elements that must be considered by any writer, new or published. These elements apply to screenwriters as well.

- Is your book or movie more **character** or more **plot-driven**?
- What is the **genre** of your book or movie?
- What about **names** for your characters?
- Whose **point of view** guides the story?

Whether you are a dedicated writer of copious outlines or whether you write each page by the seat of your pants without knowing what is coming next, these four questions remain important and somehow must be answered either before you sit down to write or soon after.

This book is aimed at helping those authors or screenwriters who want to publish commercial fiction or to see their work up on the silver screen. These are stories targeted to people who wish to read for entertainment. They want to forget the troubles of their everyday world and become absorbed in the story and the character's problems. Or they wish to go to a movie and be swept away from their everyday life into a land of excitement and enchantment.

To that end, we have devised a new way to build your character. It is a combination of explanations and definitions of what goes into building a character, together with checklists and exercises which will allow your characters to become real, breathing people.

We will also introduce you to the Character Diamond or the four C's, which is another way to look at character building. We have also created three characters to follow throughout the book so you can see how we have used the various steps to build these characters. Let's begin.

Building a memorable character is an ongoing PROCESS. You will discover, as you go through this book, with each new element you add to your character, s/he becomes more real, more three-dimensional, and more memorable.

WHAT COMES FIRST?

The CHARACTER or the PLOT?

The answer is — it really doesn't matter. Some writers develop characters that make the plot, while others take a plot idea and then build the characters. What matters is that the two must work together to yield a good book or movie.

No matter how great the plot, it is the characters who make the story memorable. Even a unique and original premise soon grows boring if readers or viewers don't care about the characters. On the other hand, wonderful characters can become static if they don't face some sort of interesting journey or exciting conflict to let them develop into everything they can be. In this way, plot and characters intertwine until you couldn't have one without the other.

The plot is the journey of turns and twists characters face in the pages of a book or on the frames of a movie reel. Think of it as a crusade characters set out on. Plots may have sudden and exciting adventures along the way which allow our characters to change and grow. Like each character the various turns should have a meaning in the overall flow of the story.

If the plot comes first, the writer then needs to decide on the best character or type of character to fit with that plot. In the movie *Jurassic Park*, Dr. Grant is the perfect person to put into a dinosaur setting — he's an expert. But he isn't a fan of children, so he is suddenly set into the predicament of having to lead two children to safety. In the movie and book *Rebecca*, the heroine is a simple, soft-spoken companion who is thrown into the role of mistress of a great house — Manderley — once run by the beautiful and confident Rebecca.

The plot turns in both of these works have the reader or viewer on the edge of their seats, but the characters and plot must both mesh before a wonderful story emerges.

When the characters come first, the plot hinges on the character's actions and how they will cope with the various problems thrown at them. In *Jurassic Park*, Dr. Grant must save the children and he finds they can be resourceful partners. In *Rebecca*, the reader probably wouldn't have related to the heroine if she'd been every bit as beautiful or poised as her dead rival.

So what makes a character memorable?

Is it the life adventure that she or he is forced to journey through, or is it how the character grows and changes along the story path? We, the reader or viewer, become emotionally entwined with her or his problems while hoping that the hero/heroine will find the solution to the dilemma and save the day.

When the plot comes first:
- The idea of the story forms from an article about a murder case, or an incident from real life. Things like a divorce or death may force the main character to cope. Here the plot is determined by what type of character is needed to fit the action of the story.

When the character comes first:
- You're reading the biography of the first man or woman who did something outrageous, when suddenly you think, *What if I put this character in another situation?* The character is driving the story and what s/he wants or what emotional or physical baggage s/he brings along also helps determine the plot.

The character changes as the plot grows. Plot and character are inseparable.

However, in the end, it is the character who the reader or viewer remembers no matter which idea came to the author first.

Here are a few of our most memorable characters — characters that remain in our hearts and minds long after the book is read or the movie has been seen.

BOOKS
- **Sherlock Holmes** by Sir Arthur Conan Doyle
- **Harry Potter** and his friends in the *Harry Potter* series by J. K. Rowling
- **Ebenezer Scrooge** in *A Christmas Carol* by Charles Dickens
- **Frodo Baggins** in *The Lord of the Rings* Trilogy by J.R.R. Tolkien
- **Emma Woodehouse** in *Emma* by Jane Austen
- **Tom Joad** in *The Grapes of Wrath* by John Steinbeck
- **Edmond Dantes** as *The Count of Monte Cristo* by Alexandre Dumas
- **Bridget Jones** in *Bridget Jones's Diary* by Helen Fielding
- **Cyrano de Bergerac** by Edmond Rostand
- **Stephanie Plum** by Janet Evanovitch from the Stephanie Plum series

MOVIES
- **Sergeant Martin Riggs** (Mel Gibson) in *Lethal Weapon*
- **Mary Poppins** (Julie Andrews) in *Mary Poppins*
- **Charlie Allnut** (Humphrey Bogart) in *The African Queen*
- **Annie Wilkes** (Kathy Bates) in *Misery*
- **Raymond Babbitt** (Dustin Hoffman) in *Rain Man*
- **Don Vito Corleone** (Marlon Brando) in *The Godfather*
- **Vivian Ward** (Julia Roberts) in *Pretty Woman*
- **Han Solo** (Harrison Ford) in the *Star Wars* sagas
- **Dolly Levi** (Barbra Streisand) in *Hello Dolly*
- **Mark Thackeray** (Sidney Poitier) in *To Sir, With Love*
- **Charlotte Vale** (Bette Davis) in *Now, Voyager*
- **Mona Lisa Vito** (Marisa Tomei) in *My Cousin Vinny*
- **Captain Marko Ramius** (Sean Connery) in *The Hunt for Red October*
- **Del Spooner** (Will Smith) in *I, Robot*
- **Matron Mama Morton** (Queen Latifah) in *Chicago*
- **Marshal Samuel Gerard** (Tommy Lee Jones) in *The Fugitive*
- **Captain Jack Sparrow** (Johnny Depp) in *Pirates of the Caribbean*

TV SERIES
- **Londo Mollari** (Peter Jurasik) in *Babylon 5*
- **Hercule Poirot** (David Suchet) in *Hercule Poirot*
- **Lucy (Lucille Ball)** in *I Love Lucy*
- **Lt. Commander Data** (Brent Spiner) in *Star Trek*
- **Murphy Brown** (Candace Bergen) in *Murphy Brown*
- **Al Bundy** (Ed O'Neil) in *Married...with Children*
- **Gil Grissom** (William Peterson) in *CSI*
- **Thurston Howell III** (Jim Backus) in *Gilligan's Island*
- **Alan Harper** (Jon Cryer) in *Two and a Half Men*

PLAYS
- **Enrique Claudin** in *The Phantom of the Opera* by Andrew Lloyd Webber
- **Harold Hill** in *The Music Man* by Meredith Wilson

DECIDING ON A GENRE

According to the Romance Writers of America (RWA) almost 40 percent of all fiction books sold are some type of romance. Action, suspense, and mystery all come in a distant second, third, and fourth.

It is advisable, if you wish to be published, to write a story in the genre that you most enjoy reading. Find out who is publishing that type of book. You wouldn't send a pure science fiction or a horror story to Harlequin Romance because they publish romance exclusively.

Check out the Web sites of the different publishers to see what their specialties are and read over their submission guidelines. This step alone will put you in front of the thousands of other emerging writers who mistakenly think they can do things "their way."

In the romance genre there are a couple dozen sub-genres. Here are a few:

- Romantic suspense where not only the hero and heroine fall in love but they must work out their problems amid a background of danger and suspense
- The modern fairy tale which dictates that true love will prevail
- Red hot erotica
- Chick-lit
- Historical
- Inspirational

Each genre and even its sub-genre has its own rules, word count, and degree of sexual tension and sensuality. There will be little in an inspirational novel while the pages of an erotic novel sizzle. The heroes and heroines can be any age — from an older hero with naive heroine, to older protagonists finding love the second time around.

In the beginning, when the character and the genre meet, certain details about the character become evident.

For example, if the genre is a medical thriller, the hero/heroine most likely will be involved in the medical profession, giving them the necessary resources to solve the problem(s).

If the story is a western set in the nineteenth century, the character needs to have internal backbone as well as the physical attributes to survive a hostile environment.

On the following pages are some main genres with examples taken from books, movies, and TV. We have also listed authors who write in a specific genre.

Deciding on a Genre

We will use **ROMANTIC SUSPENSE** as our genre, because it contains both the love interest as well as the mystery aspect we enjoy in our stories.

We will start with a **HERO,** tall, dark, and handsome, of course,

add a **HEROINE,** who is just an average woman in her late twenties, and...

drum roll...
create a nasty **VILLAIN.**

NOTE: One editor, when asked what she looked for first in a new writer's submission, replied...

"The more effective query letter is one that states, up front, what genre the story is in."

GENRES

Action — *action and adventure scenes in which the protagonists are trying to reach a goal through often perilous means and are confronted by numerous obstacles along the way.*

Sub-genres: Chase - Quest - Disasters, natural or otherwise

Books	**Movies**	**TV**	**Authors**
• *Ice Station Zebra*	• *Seven Years in Tibet*	• *Tarzan*	• Ian Fleming
• *The Watchers*	• *The Fugitive*	• *Xena Warrior Princess*	• Michael Crichton
• *Cain*	• *Die Hard*	• *Walker, Texas Ranger*	• Roderick Thorp
• *Patriot Games*	• *Count of Monte Cristo*	• *MacGyver*	• James Patterson

Crime — *the solving of a murder or major crime wherein each sub-genre has its own special guidelines. Usually filled with plenty of inside details.*

Sub-genres: Hard-Boiled Detective Stories - Police procedure - Forensic

Books	**Movies**	**TV**	**Authors**
• *Mildred Pierce*	• *Seven*	• *The Sopranos*	• Micky Spillane
• *The Wishing Game*	• *Lethal Weapon*	• *Law and Order*	• Ed McBain
• *Cold Service*	• *Fargo*	• *CSI*	• Thomas Harris
• *The Silence of the Lambs*	• *Papparazzi*	• *Perry Mason*	• Kathy Reichs

Erotica — *sex plays a definitive part of the story.*

Books	**Movies**	**TV**	**Authors**
• *Valley of the Dolls*	• *Basic Instinct*	• *Desperate Housewives*	• D. H. Lawrence
• *Lady Chatterly's Lover*	• *Last Tango in Paris*	• *Sex and the City*	• Henry Miller
• *Diary of Anais Nin*	• *Dressed to Kill*	• *Red Shoe Diaries*	• Ann Rice
• *Fear of Flying*	• *Body Double*	• *Taxicab Confessions*	• James Joyce

Fantasy — *a departure from reality in an imaginary world often peopled with characters such as fairies, leprechauns, talking animals, or humans imbued with fantastic powers or abilities.*

Sub-genres: Fairy Tales - Mythology - Super Heroes

Books	**Movies**	**TV**	**Authors**
• *Cinderella*	• *Harry Potter*	• *Buffy the Vampire Slayer*	• J. K. Rowling
• *The Borrowers*	• *The Princess Bride*	• *Bewitched*	• William Goldman
• *The Neverending Story*	• *Lord of the Rings*	• *Charmed*	• J. R. R. Tolkien
• *Elfstones of Shannara*	• *Freaky Friday*	• *Sabrina*	• Michael Ende

GENRES

Historical — *set in a well-defined period with accurate historical details.*
Sub-genres: Regency - Civil War - American West - Scottish Highlands

Books	**Movies**	**TV**	**Authors**
• *Gone With the Wind*	• *Valmont*	• *Poirot*	• James Michener
• *A Tale of Two Cities*	• *Tom Jones*	• *China Beach*	• Jane Austen
• *The Black Flower*	• *The Scarlet Letter*	• *Little House on the Prairie*	• Nathaniel Hawthorne
• *The House of Seven Gables*	• *Alexander the Great*	• *Dr. Quinn, Medicine Woman*	• Leon Uris

Horror — *designed to invoke intense fear and repugnance, and often involving supernatural phenomenon.*
Sub-genres: Vampires - Werewolves - Ghosts - Paranormal events

Books	**Movies**	**TV**	**Authors**
• *Dracula*	• *The Watchers*	• *The Outer Limits*	• Dean Koontz
• *Frankenstein*	• *Friday the 13th*	• *Angel*	• Anne Rice
• *Amazon*	• *Signs*	• *The Twilight Zone*	• Stephen King
• *Dead as a Doornail*	• *Halloween*	• *Tales from the Crypt*	• Peter Straub

Inspirational — *a message of hope, faith restored or regained, intending to inspire the reader.*

Books	**Movies**	**TV**	**Authors**
• *Christie*	• *It's a Wonderful Life*	• *Touched by an Angel*	• Gregory Allen Howard
• *A Man Called Peter*	• *Dead Poet's Society*	• *Highway to Heaven*	• Gale Sayers
• *A Boy Called It*	• *Finding Forrester*	• *Joan of Arcadia*	• Tom Schulman
• *Brian's Song*	• *Oh, God*	• *7th Heaven*	• Mike Rick

Mystery/Suspense — *uncovering and piecing together clues to solve a mystery, murder, or lost person.*
Sub-genres: Private or Amateur Detective - Cozies - Courtroom dramas - Mysteries with a comic edge such as *Columbo*

Books	**Movies**	**TV**	**Authors**
• *Maltese Falcon*	• *Ten Little Indians*	• *Diagnosis Murder*	• Agatha Christie
• *A is for Alibi*	• *To Catch a Thief*	• *Law and Order*	• Janet Evanovich
• *Along Came a Spider*	• *The Big Sleep*	• *Murder, She Wrote*	• Dashiell Hammett
• *The Hound of the Baskervilles*	• *Notorious*	• *Monk*	• Richard Condon

GENRES

Romance — *a happily-ever-after love story with an optimistic and emotionally satisfying ending.*
Sub-genres: Romantic Suspense or Comedy - Chick-lit - Historical

Books	Movies	TV	Authors
• Rebecca	• Sleepless in Seattle	• I Love Lucy	• Sandra Brown
• Sense and Sensibility	• Indiscreet	• The Love Boat	• Nora Roberts
• Wuthering Heights	• Ghost	• Dharma and Greg	• Janet Oakes
• Bridget Jones's Diary	• Romancing the Stone	• Friends	• Jayne Anne Krentz

Science Fiction — *set in the future or on other worlds. Often features space travel or futuristic devices.*
Sub-genres: Paranormal - Supernatural - Time travel

Books	Movies	TV	Authors
• Mona Lisa Overdrive	• Terminator	• Star Trek	• Arthur C. Clark
• The Martian Chronicles	• X-Men	• Battlestar Galactica	• Philip K. Dick
• Battlefield Earth	• The Matrix	• Babylon 5	• H. G. Wells
• The Hitchhiker's Guide to the Galaxy	• Alien	• Stargate SG-1	• Robert Heinlein

Thriller — *designed to evoke great excitement, trepidation, and intense sensations.*
Sub-genres: Spy and/or espionage - Medical and Legal

Books	Movies	TV	Authors
• Coma	• Panic Room	• The Avengers	• Lisa Gardner
• The General's Daughter	• True Lies	• Cold Case Files	• Clive Cussler
• Suspect	• The Eiger Sanction	• La Femme Nikita	• John Grisham
• The DaVinci Code	• The Bourne Identity	• Alias	• Tom Clancy

Westerns — *a western setting about cowboys or frontier life either contemporary or historical.*

Books	Movies	TV	Authors
• The Gunslinger	• Mask of Zorro	• Wild Wild West	• Louis L'Amour
• Lonesome Dove	• Tombstone	• Gunsmoke	• Ralph Cotlon
• Lone Star Rising	• Quigley Down Under	• Bonanza	• Tony Hillerman
• Riders of the Purple Sage	• El Diablo	• The Big Valley	• John Meston

DECIDING ON A CHARACTER'S NAME

As Shakespeare asked in *Romeo and Juliet*, "What's in a name?"

Everything!

What you name your characters can be helpful in determining a personality trait, creating a flaw the character needs to overcome, or an ingrained point of conflict with another character.

Names do not have to be complicated or strange. Start with what you know about your story, or your character. Is she or he from a particular country? A particular ethnic background? A precise time period?

Perhaps your major female character has a German background. Check out a German name Web site or open your baby name book to the section on girls' names and go through the pages until you find a name that appeals to you.

For example, toward the end of the "R's" there are three possibilities, *Roderica, Rolanda, and Rosamond.* Is your heroine royal? *Roderica* means "famous ruler." This name would work well in a fantasy or fairy-tale type story. What if *Roderica* needs to claim her throne? What if *Roderica* is not really "famous" but rather "infamous?" What did she do or not do to gain this reputation?

Rolanda means "fame of the land." Hmmm. What land is *Rolanda* famous in? What did she do to become famous? Win a Miss Universe title? What problems could develop for her region because she's made the area famous? Sometimes name books have other derivations. The name *Rosamond* is related to the name *Roz*. Not only does *Roz* sound contemporary, but also, *Roz* means a "famous guardian." Oh boy, now that opens up some possibilities. What if *Roz* has to protect the president? What if *Roz* had a huge failure in her past? What if *Roz* needs to train to be a guardian? What if *Roz* has no talent at being a guardian and she has to fill the position?

The possibilities are endless.

Many novels have villains. The name choice for this person should fit the depth of his or her villainy. A grasp of current events and history is helpful. We aren't likely to see an Attila, Benedict, or even an Adolph used as the average reader has clear associations to these historical names.

One last thought about villains. Not always do they have to be human beings or even alive. So if an alien, animal, or entity is present in your story choose the name carefully to reflect some aspect of the being.

On the next page we have listed a few suggestions for you to consider as you develop your character's name.

Naming Our Characters

The first problem we have when developing characters is naming our people.

Since this is a contemporary novel, the names should reflect the times and the personality of each character.

The heroine is shy, but during the course of the tale will become bold and even daring.

The letter "K" has a nice firm ring to it...how about **KAYLA**?

Now the hero.

QUINN is a strong-sounding name.

For the villain, let's be daring and make our villain a villainess, a character no one would ever suspect. She needs a friendly name.

EMILY is a good old-fashioned name. Sweet and unassuming. Perfect for a killer.

To recap...

KAYLA is the heroine
QUINN is the hero
and
EMILY is the villainess.

NAMING YOUR CHARACTER
General Guidelines

Resources:
- The Web. Go to any search engine and put in "names." Thousands of sites will pop up, not only from different parts of the world, but from different time periods in history.
- Phonebooks and baby-naming books are useful as well as genealogical and historical references.

Gender:
- Check to see if the name is appropriate for the gender of your character.
- If a name such as *Alex, Bobbie, Fletcher*, or even *Sammy* can signify either sex, have a very good reason for giving your character this name because it could confuse the reader.

Setting:
- Be sure the name is appropriate for the setting. Does *Debbie* evoke the image of a Viking maiden? Which sounds more like a cowboy, *Wolfgang* or *Jake*?

Time Period:
- Each time period had favorite names that immediately put the reader in that age. *Charlotte* or *Victoria* evokes eighteenth-century England, while *Jennifer* or *Kaitlin* is more contemporary.

Personality:
- An *Elmer* or a *Lamar* could possibly be a hero, but if you pin one of these names on your hero, it might give the reader an image of a "Barney Fife" kind of character. Giving your hero a name like *Nick* or *Max* brings to mind an image of a strong, brooding hero.
- Could the name, like a nickname, signal some kind of a character trait? *Shorty* or *Red* can be used to develop either a distasteful or charming person. Perhaps a perfectly great name such as *Gabrielle* may become simply *Gabby*...so does this gal talk a lot?

Other Considerations:
- Don't make your names too difficult to pronounce. You want your reader to remember your characters, not abbreviate their names to "that guy whose name started with T."
- If at all possible, dodge common names like *John* or *Mary*, especially if they are villains.
- Try to use names that start with different letters in the alphabet. *Amanda* and *Annabelle*, although charming names for sisters, are confusing to readers. Which one is the heroine?
- How the names sound is important. If the character is arrogant, use a hard consonant, such as D or hard G. Remember Gaston in *Beauty and the Beast*?
- Does the name "feel" right for both the character and the genre?
- Finally, don't name every character that walks into your story. Minor characters can best be described by their occupation, i.e., the cook, the butler, or the teacher. When you name a character, you indicate this person is important and will have a significant role in the story.

WHOSE STORY IS IT? POV

Understanding Point of View (POV) can be a bit tricky. POV is simply telling the story from one character's perspective. This means knowing what that character is thinking and feeling as the action takes place. It is literally "getting into that character's head" and seeing the story through his or her eyes.

There are three major types of POV:

- First person
- Third person
- Omniscient

First person is the easiest to understand and probably the most difficult to master. This method tells the story as though the writer is the character. Often it is used in mysteries or in the popular "chick-lit" genre. "I,"as the narrator, tells the story. Characters like Janet Evanovich's *Stephanie Plum* or Sue Grafton's *Kinsey Millhone* tell their stories in first person. On television, Carrie Bradshaw basically told the story of her friends and her life in *Sex and the City*.

Third person is the POV used in most popular fiction, with the author focusing on one or more characters, and then telling the story from a particular character's point of view. Too many points of view can be confusing and lead to "head hopping" where the reader has difficulty tracking who is really telling the story.

Using third person, the reader is given one character's emotions and thoughts in a scene. Readers view the action through that character's eyes. This can be particularly useful in building suspense if the villain is plotting something dire against the hero or heroine and the reader knows it, but the characters don't.

In a romance, often the heroine's thoughts will be told and then later, the reader will learn why the hero reacted a certain way when the POV shifts to his side.

Omniscient point of view lets the writer tell the story so that the reader knows all and the writer tells all. This is seen most often in literary works. It is often compared to being like "God" in your story.

Whoever is telling the story, the writer needs to remember to put the POV into the hands of the character who has the most to gain or lose in each scene.

It makes each scene stronger and more vivid in the mind of the reader if only one POV is used in the entire scene.

First person

- I said

    The sun slowly sank below the horizon. I had never seen such vivid colors before and wondered why I didn't come to the beach more often.

Third person

- She said

    She watched the sun slowly sink below the horizon and wondered why she didn't come to the beach more often

Omniscient

- God said

    The sun sank slowly below the horizon. The girl watching looked pleased with the view as if she had never seen a sunset before.

POV

As the POV changes, the story changes. The writer should decide whose scene it is.

The differences between the sexes and their POV:

*   Women see the world through an array of vivid emotions
    Huge crocodile tears rolled down her cheeks as she learned of her grandfather's death knowing that she had been too busy, too involved with her own life, to visit him over the past few months.

*   Men view the world through their actions
    Upon hearing of his grandfather's death, he began making the funeral arrangements.

*   Women make suggestions
    She smiled shyly as she glanced at her lover and asked, "Why don't we have lunch now?"

*   Men make statements
    "Let's go to lunch," he said starting to leave the room.

*   Women tend to be more emotional in their statements.
    "I hope Helen is in a good mood. I get so frustrated when she starts on one of her rants."

*   Men tend to be more factual and logical in their statements.
    "Have you thought about what will happen if you go to Helen's?"

How do you determine which character's POV is best to use?

*   Choose the character who has the most to lose in the scene, not the character who has the most to gain.

*   If you've having trouble deciding, try writing the scene in first person
    first in one character's POV,
    then do the scene, still in first person, in the other character's POV.

*   Or if you still can't decide,
    try the scene in the POV of the character who is simply observing an emotional crisis involving the other character.

Check the publisher you are targeting concerning POV considerations.

For example, LUNA, a female-focused fantasy line from Harlequin/Silhouette books, uses primarily the POV of the female protagonist. Also in Red Dress Ink, a line of Harlequin/Silhouette books, there is no restriction on POV, but they do require a strong female protagonist.

Some mysteries including a variety of detective stories and chick-lit novels in particular are written in first person POV. In Harlequin Next they require a strong secondary cast and plot but they are open to first person POV if it fits the story.

OUR STORY — A ROMANTIC SUSPENSE PLOT

We have made up a Romantic Suspense story with a love interest between Kayla and Quinn. The suspense is created by Emily as the killer.

KAYLA Turner *(the heroine)* intends to leave her husband. She has packed her suitcases and put them in the car along with her plane ticket. She drives to the hospital where he is a nurse in the trauma unit to tell him she is leaving.

He is quite competent but is an opportunist. He sees an opportunity in his boss, Dr. **EMILY Minton** *(the villain),* who heads up the trauma unit.

One night, a patient is brought into the trauma unit after being involved in a car accident. Emily kills the man because she feels his injuries are so severe he will be in a coma the rest of his life.

Kayla's husband confronts Emily and asks her for an outrageous amount of money to keep quiet.

Thinking quickly, Emily also kills him, then careful to leave no forensic evidence behind, goes home.

A few minutes later, Kayla comes looking for her husband at the hospital. She goes to the doctor's lounge and finds his body. She rushes to his side. As she is kneeling, someone walks in and sees her with blood on her hands.

The police are called and the homicide detective in charge is **QUINN Salazar** *(the hero)*. All the evidence points to Kayla being the murderer. She was found leaning over the body with her hand on the murder weapon. Her prints are the only ones on the weapon. The police think she planned to stop at the hospital, kill her husband, then head straight for the airport and her flight out of the country.

This is a quick and very sketchy plot outline, but we need to have some idea of what elements to bring or add to each character.

For example, if we know that Quinn is the detective, we can almost see his character develop before our eyes. Kayla, on the other hand, we need to work with a bit more because, at this stage of the game, we are really not sure how her character will develop and change. Emily is pure evil. That is about all we know about her. She will be a challenge to create.

On the following page, we have taken these three characters and put them in all the different genres to show you how they might change when the genre changes. You might want to do this with your characters until you are sure the character and the genre are a perfect fit.

GENRES

Following are simple examples of how your characters will change when put into a different genre. Note that the genre actually "molds" to some degree how the character will develop or the character will define the genre. During the course of developing your story, you might find what had originally been planned as a Romance now has become a Fantasy, because of changes you've made as you developed your characters.

Action — Kayla's quest is to find the killer. Quinn will help her, but the villainess puts various obstacles in their path, such as a bomb in their car, or setting fire to Kayla's house.

Crime — Here Quinn is the lead character and a recovering alcoholic detective. While following the clues, Kayla becomes important to him. Emily covers up her illegal activities.

Erotica — Kayla and Quinn's physical attraction is paramount and the mystery secondary. Setting and sensual details are very important.

Fantasy — Emily is a fire-breathing dragon. Kayla is a mystical being (elf) and Quinn is a knight or a sorcerer.

Historical — In a Regency, Kayla is the daughter of the local vicar, while Quinn is the nobleman. Emily, the sister of Quinn's best friend is vying for Quinn's proposal and tries to discredit Kayla.

Horror — Emily is a vampire on the hunt for a mate. Quinn is a vampire hunter, while Kayla is Emily's next chosen victim.

Inspirational — Quinn has lost faith. Kayla is a new minister in a small town. Emily is Quinn's ex-wife, now remarried and threatening to overturn the court decision and take their five-year son into her custody.

Mystery/Suspense — No one, not even the reader, knows who the killer is. Kayla is trying to keep the killer from striking again and asks Quinn to help her.

Romance — Kayla and Quinn, although they have conflicting ideals, fall in love. Emily is the jealous woman next door, staking her claim on Quinn.

Science Fiction — Emily is a shape shifter from another planet determined to find out if earth would make a habitable world for her race. Quinn is a scientist trying to prevent worldwide holocaust. Kayla discovers Emily's agenda.

Thriller — Emily, a doctor, is a serial killer in a medical setting. Quinn is also a doctor and works at the same hospital as Emily. Kayla, a nurse, begins to suspect that one of these two doctors is the killer.

Western — In a frontier setting, Quinn becomes the sheriff, Kayla the daughter of a poor rancher, and Emily is the nasty wife of the local, rich land baron.

Remember, there is no one way to mold your character. Everyone builds their character in a slightly different way.

It's okay to start with Step One but it's perfectly all right to start with Step Eight or Nine.

There is no one way to read this book. Some like to read the sidebars first, while others will want to do all the exercises first.

Once again, it's your book. Read and use it any way you want.

HOW TO BEST USE THIS BOOK

We suggest a fast read through of the whole book to see exactly what is covered and for you to decide what characters from which story you are considering working with, or if you want to start with fresh characters.

As you follow our three characters, which are on the left page, you will be able to create your three characters in the worksheet provided on the right-hand page.

We hope this book will help you in your endeavor to write authentic and memorable characters. As we wrote and edited this book, we kept saying to each other, "I wish I had known all of this when I first started writing."

We have tried to include everything we have learned over the years about crafting exciting and well-rounded characters. Between the four of us, this book is the result of more than fifty years of "I've been there and done that," sometimes with great results and at other times with much rewriting.

May this book help you to breathe life into characters who will leap off the page and as a result, all of your stories will be million-dollar winners!

We sincerely wish you the very best with your career.

Sue Viders
Lucynda Storey
Cher Gorman
Becky Martinez
Denver, Colorado

PHYSICAL DESCRIPTION

OVERVIEW

Your character walks into a room. What is the immediate impression he conveys? Yes, what he's wearing has something to do with this, but look deeper. Do his broad shoulders tell the reader he can carry any load? Does his long, blond hair convey he's a rebel? The choices you make about a character's body and looks will help the reader relate to him or her.

Age

First, determine the age of your character. That will give the reader more insight into how and why the character will act and react in your story.

Physique

Define your character's physical attributes. Look at the overall body type of your character. How tall is she? Does she have skinny legs that were the bane of her existence when she was a kid? Is she round and short, a roly-poly kind of girl? Does he have an artist's hands that he uses to great effect when he's speaking passionately about a political issue? Or are his hands hard and calloused from working on a pirate ship?

Face

It's been written a single face launched a thousand ships. The combination of a dark brow and grim mouth have frightened many a maiden, while bright eyes and a dimpled cheek have enticed many a lad. Details count. Each small choice can emotionally impact the character and thus the reader.

Distinguishing Characteristics

These are the unique physical aspects that make your character stand out. Does he limp from an old injury when it's cold? When he's angry do white lines show around his mouth? Does she have the wide, sexy mouth of her Italian mother's ancestry? Does her blonde hair and white skin embarrass her in the hot, summer months because she gets sunburned so easily?

Some of the more basic information you will need to decide include:
- Age
- Height
- Weight
- Ethnicity
- Hair
- Eyes

Heroine - Kayla

Kayla is 28 and has been a homemaker since getting married.

Why is this important?

Her age shows the reader/ viewer that she is young and will probably make mistakes while trying to clear her name.

Hero - Quinn

Quinn is 35 and has been a detective for the past 8 years.

Why is this important?

He has to have had enough experience to solve this murder, and have seen enough murder cases to react to evidence.

Villain - Emily

Emily is 43. She has to be this age since she is a surgeon and needed ten years in medical school, then internship, etc.

Why is this important?

She needs to be this age to have the experience to be the department head.

AGE

All characters have an age and a date of birth. Determining the age of your characters intertwines with their education and profession. A seasoned police officer will not have the youthfulness and lack of experience a rookie will. Many a police saga has played the knowledgeable, wiser cop against the younger, brash newbie who still needs to learn the ropes. Think of movies like *LA Confidential* or *Lethal Weapon*.

Age can make a difference in how the story develops. If the hero or heroine is younger maybe they think they know it all only to learn they don't. Perhaps your older character is jaded or cynical yet learns to love again, or finds he still cares about his life. Age groups can vary from infant, to teenager, to young adults, to middle-aged adults and finally to seniors. Each group has its own characteristics and their its own audience.

Check out prospective publishers and their guidelines as to age groups that best suit their publishing needs. For example, if writing an action movie script aimed at teenage boys and young adult males, your hero might be a shy high school student, such as Peter Parker in *Spiderman*.

Giving your characters a date of birth allows you to use their horoscope to indicate a particular personality trait. For example, Leos are thought to be leaders while Pisces are supposed to be artistic. By checking the various horoscopes you can get great ideas about your characters.

While the actual birth date may never be revealed in the course of the story an author can use the information to add dimension to the character. Birthdays are a big deal. Is one of your characters turning thirty? Will there be a big surprise party and lots of fun or is this person depressed because life is passing her or him by and she or he needs to do something drastic?

EXERCISES

- He is going to be 35 next month and his family is concerned that he is not married. As an heir to the throne, he needs a wife, but she cannot be some simpering young miss just out of the schoolroom. What are his options?

- In the movie *Freaky Friday*, the fortyish mother and the teenager change places. The comedy comes from what is expected in each age group. Now your hero, age 52, a scientist, creates an anti-aging formula that makes him 25 years younger. What happens to him?

- She was born on Christmas Day. How has this affected her life?

Heroine

Name:

Age:

Why is this important?

Hero

Name:

Age:

Why is this important?

Villain

Name:

Age:

Why is this important?

Heroine - Kayla

Kayla is five feet, six inches, slightly above average. She's curvy in the right places, but thinks she's overweight.

Why is this important?

She is overly sensitive about her weight (thanks to her husband) but hates to exercise. She would rather lose the weight by simply not eating fattening foods...but she loves ice cream.

Hero - Quinn

Quinn is tall, a bit over six feet, physically fit, and athletic.

Why is this important?

Quinn lives a spartan lifestyle and is extremely disciplined about exercise. He's not concerned with how he looks, but how he feels physically.

Villain - Emily

Emily is petite with a delicate and well-toned build.

Why is this important?

This gives others like Quinn the impression she is on the "helpless" side and needs protecting.

PHYSIQUE

He is a brute of a man. Big, tall, and strong. The reader immediately begins to form an image of your character and also starts to make assumptions about his background, his personality, and his attitude.

As a writer you need to be aware of these conclusions and use them wisely in furthering your story and in defining your character. Besides the character's age, you will need to know the character's height, weight, ethnic background, possible health or medical problems and their overall appearance.

Besides the physical aspects of how a body looks, consider how it smells. Is it clean, with a great soap scent or does the smoke from her cigarettes permeate her clothes? How does his body feel? Smooth as a baby's bottom or tough from years of hard labor? What color is his skin tone? Tan from too much sun or pale white?

Don't neglect to use choices you make about his physique in the actual writing of your story. Is this man's dominating size used to intimidate? Does he use it as a powerful tool like Superman? Does it define his personality? Is he as tough on the inside as he is on the outside? Or is he more like Shrek, tough on the outside, but a softie underneath?

How does the character feel about his or her body? Is she ashamed of it because she is overweight or proud that she is an Amazon? Is he careful not to let anyone see how his crippled leg hurts or how he limps so badly he never leaves his house?

Surprise, outwit, and entertain your reader by using the character's physique in every way you can.

EXERCISES

- Think of Arnold Schwarzenegger in any of his movies. How, or in what way, was his physique important to the story?

- This character doesn't work out. He's not an athlete, but a couch potato. Now, a doctor has told this person to exercise and lose weight. How does this person decide to go about changing his or her physique?

- What about the lead character in *Bridget Jones's Diary?* Would her character have been as believable if she were thin? Why not?

Heroine

Name:

Physique:

Why is this important?

Hero

Name:

Physique:

Why is this important?

Villain

Name:

Physique:

Why is this important?

Heroine - Kayla

Kayla does not consider herself pretty. She has red hair, green eyes, and a peaches-and-cream complexion. She never bothers with makeup.

Why is this important?

She's shy, so she's not trying to impress anyone. You have to get to know her before her inner beauty shines through.

Hero - Quinn

Quinn has a broken nose and a military-style haircut. His face is clean shaven and he gets a haircut every two weeks.

Why is this important?

It reflects his disciplined life and he's been in scrapes before.

Villain - Emily

Emily has an oval-shaped face, with short brown hair and amber-colored cat eyes. Her left eye has a slight twitch, which is only noticeable when she is angry.

Why is this important?

Her innocence and average appearance hide her dark side.

FACE

Just to say that your heroine is beautiful does not truly convey what she looks like. Every reader has a different mental picture of what beautiful means. You need to be more specific.

Are her eyes brown or hazel or the color of a mountain lake on a clear summer day? Are his eyes the deep blue of a peaceful ocean or the deeper blue of a turbulent sea? Can you actually describe the color of one's eyes without using the actual color? And are those eyes large, hostile, probing, owlish, or perhaps hidden behind wire-rimmed spectacles? Glasses are often used when the characters need to disguise themselves when investigating a crime or escaping from the villain.

Speaking of glasses, consider the time period of your story. Spectacles, monocles, and a quizzing glass primarily used in the 17th century, are quite different from lenses that are permanently implanted in the eyes. Laser surgery also can correct most eye problems, but contacts are still used to change the color of one's eyes.

Try to envision the scariest monster you possibly can. Think back to your childhood and pick out every ugly aspect of that monster. A hairy beard? Dark, piercing eyes? A broad face and thick nostrils, better to blow your house down? Does his long hair strike fear into your heart? You might be describing a fierce villain, but you could also be describing Harry Potter's good friend, Hagrid.

In the movie, *Hell Boy*, Ron Perlman plays a demon who protects humans from the forces of darkness. His face and eyes are red, he has two shortened horns sticking out of his forehead, black hair, and a goatee. He looked like the very devil but his character worked for the good of mankind.

EXERCISES

- Describe a beautiful woman who has interesting eyes. Is the woman a heroine or a villainess? How will the reader be able to tell this from her eyes? Should the reader be able to?

- His face was memorable. Describe a male face that will have a long-lasting impact on the reader or viewer. Remember the face doesn't necessarily have to be handsome or ugly...just memorable.

- How, or in what way, is that character's face important to the story?

Heroine

Name:

Face:

Why is this important?

Hero

Name:

Face:

Why is this important?

Villain

Name:

Face:

Why is this important?

Heroine - Kayla

Kayla's hair is overly curly and flaming red.

Why is this important?

All her life she has been teased about her hair and has been called names such as "red" and "stoplight." She would like to cut it all off and wear a wig or maybe dye it blonde. But she is afraid to do this as it might make her look guilty.

Hero - Quinn

Quinn has a scar on the side of his face from a knife cut that no longer bothers him.

Why is this important?

The scar reminds him to be cautious in his confrontations with others.

Villain - Emily

Emily has several, although faded, acne scars that she tries to cover with makeup.

Why is this important?

Her acne scars have made her self-conscious. This in turn led her to choose a career where she would be respected for her brains and not her looks.

DISTINGUISHING CHARACTERISTICS

He strides into the room on his peg leg. She limps into the room, trying to hide from all attention. His tattoo could show his love for the sea, or his desire for attention. The diamond stud in her nose could show her love of fashion or her defiant personality. Body piercing and tattoos are a need to be noticed.

What do these details have in common? They are all distinguishing characteristics. Small or large details can help convey something about your character's heart and soul, his background, or what he thinks of himself.

You will need to decide if the characteristics are:

- congenital
- the result of an injury
- deliberately chosen by the character
- the result of an illness

When you are making choices about distinguishing characteristics, try to tie these attributes to an emotional or background detail in your character's life. How did the problem occur? Have they had the problem since birth and learned to live with it, or was it from an accident and they moved past it? With these details you can expand the reader's understanding and emotional attachment to the story and the character. Each characteristic will then give depth and meaning to your story.

Some of the most memorable characters have had physical flaws. Think of Captain Hook or the Hunchback of Notre Dame. What about the Phantom of the Opera or even Cyrano de Bergerac? These are characters we remember.

EXERCISES

- A character has terrible scars somewhere on his body. How did they get there? A fire, an accident, a beating? How do these scars affect him emotionally?

- Her nose is too big for her face. Does she learn to live with it or does she have plastic surgery? Depending on what decision she makes, how does this affect her life? Was she teased during her childhood? Is she convinced she is ugly or does she carry herself with pride?

- How, or in what way, was this character's distinguishing characteristic (a large nose) important to the story? Think again of Cyrano de Bergerac.

Heroine

Name:

Distinguishing characteristic(s):

Why is this important?

Hero

Name:

Distinguishing characteristic(s):

Why is this important?

Villain

Name:

Distinguishing characteristic(s):

Why is this important?

Heroine - Kayla

Kayla is feminine in appearance. She has a nice complexion with vivid green eyes that are her best feature. Lots of curly red hair that doesn't want to be tamed. She is 28.

Why is this important?

She feels that she is average. However, she also realizes that perhaps with a bit of exercise, she might be able to make herself better looking.

Hero - Quinn

Quinn is tall and well built, and in good shape for a 35-year-old man. His face is not handsome with its broken nose, but memorable. He wears his hair short and is clean shaven. A thin white scar is all that's left of a nasty knife wound.

Why is this important?

The overall effect gives him an air of mystery and strength.

Villain - Emily

Emily is small boned but in good shape. She has short brown hair and amber-colored eyes. Her acne scars from adolescence are hardly noticeable Her only flaw is her left eye. She is 43.

Why is this important?

Her left eye will twitch slightly when she is extremely frustrated or angry. She can't seem to control it. She is self-conscious about her acne scars.

SUMMARY

Now that we have been through the various elements that make up a character's physical persona, including age, physique, face, and distinguishing characteristics, it's time to put them all together. You might want to consider keeping these details on a note card by your computer.

Remember that it is not necessary that you make special mention of the characteristics within the story and don't force them onto your character or into the story itself. Just knowing they exist can make the character come more alive in your mind and allow you to them put that feeling onto the written page. For screenwriters, remember that characteristics such as a limp or a scar on the face will be immediately visible. Think of how to develop that or use it from the first moment your audience sees the character.

Use this page to coordinate the various decisions you have made about your character. Also determine WHY these particular characteristics are vital to the story.

PROFESSION OR OCCUPATION

STEP TWO

OVERVIEW

Right or wrong, many people are defined by their profession or occupation: *"He's a doctor,"* or *"She's a ballet dancer."* Immediately, a certain image springs to mind. Perhaps he's a forest ranger. A picture of a rugged individual surfaces. Or if she is a yoga instructor, another image forms.

What your character does for a living is not only part of the physical description of the story line, but can add to the emotional turmoil and conflict the character usually has to resolve. Carefully selecting your hero and heroine's job adds another dimension to creating a memorable character.

Work Ethic

Whether born to wealth or poverty, how a character develops his or her work habits can play an important part of the story, including the conflict with either the love interest or the villain. Is your character lazy or hard-working? Anxious to succeed or simply doesn't care? Passed-over for promotion or a rising corporate star?

Profession or Occupation

Depending on the genre and the time frame of the story, your character may or may not have a choice on what he or she does for a living. A nobleman, born to wealth in the seventeenth century, has a different set of options than the son of a middle-class family or someone born in the slums of a major twenty-first century city.

Education plays an important role, but the choice of an occupation is also influenced by family, cultural environment, and the ambition of the character.

The wonderful thing about fiction is that you, the writer, can play around with all these variables until you have the perfect job for your character. Choose an occupation that gives the characters a special ability in relation to the plot. Use his or her profession to get the job done, whether it is solving a murder mystery, finding the lost city or treasure, or simply teaching a deaf child how to survive in a hostile environment.

In today's society, any profession or occupation can be performed by either sex...

but not so, if one writes historicals of any kind. In many societies, the individual is simply born into a "class" that has only so many job opportunities for women and men.

Various ethnic groups, or fantasy or futuristic societies, have different concepts of what type of work is "suitable" for each sex, age group, and class.

Heroine - Kayla
Kayla doesn't have a strong work history. One semester short of graduating from college, she was married.
Why is this important?
She has never worked outside the home and she's never finished an important project.

Hero - Quinn
Quinn works hard and often takes double shifts.
Why is this important?
He is obsessed with getting the "bad" guys. Also working hard doesn't give him free time for other pursuits like dating or a serious relationship.

Villain - Emily
Emily limits her patient load, working only three days a week.
Why is this important?
She needs the other days for herself as she needs lots of "down" time. A perfectionist, she needs time to unwind after her operations.

WORK ETHIC

How one approaches work is usually a combination of upbringing, a value system, and outside economic situations. When tied together these factors help determine a character's work ethic.

A doctor, dentist, or lawyer in today's society needs a certain amount of formal education, whereas a gang leader, jewel thief, or cab driver may simply learn as they go.

A junior executive, mercenary, or public relations specialist sometimes "apprentice" themselves with a mentor to help them master their job or occupation and work their way up the "ranks." Others might sleep their way to the top.

Why are some characters dedicated to working an eighteen-hour day while others barely work at all? Once the writer makes a firm decision in regard to each character's work ethic, it's time to give the characters a good "kick in the pants" by changing their status quo.

Putting together two opposite work ethics can be part of the conflict in the story. For example, if the hero is somewhat of a daydreamer and he falls for a gal who is extremely diligent overachiever, the sparks will fly.

Or how about a woman executive who picks other people's brains and has a secretary who has elbow grease determination. Sound like a good plot? They did in it in *Working Girl*.

Through the story, the writer must show how the character changes, grows, and evolves. Use or alter a character's work ethic to help show those changes.

EXERCISES

- This character, who has a routine job, is suddenly accused of a crime. What is the job and how will she use her work to investigate the situation?

- This character has never worked. Born to a noble family, he is in line to inherit so why does he have to do anything but party? How can the writer get this playboy to become a responsible individual, who contributes to society instead of being irresponsible?

- Describe the character's work ethic in a book you have just read or movie you really liked that became a vital part of the story. Why was his or her work ethic important to the story line? In other words, how did it help them solve the crime?

Heroine

Character:

Work ethic:

Hero

Character:

Work ethic:

Villain

Character:

Work ethic:

Heroine - Kayla

Kayla has never had a paying job of any kind. Her husband wanted her to stay at home.

Why is this important?

She has no self-confidence about finding a job or a work history for a resume.

Hero - Quinn

Quinn is a homicide detective, working his way up through the ranks.

Why is this important?

He will have the resources, contacts, and experience to help solve the murder.

Villain - Emily

Emily is a noted emergency doctor who heads up the hospital's trauma unit.

Why is this important?

By working in the trauma unit she is able to determine who will live or die.

PROFESSION OR OCCUPATION

Most people are defined by their occupations or professions.

How the character chooses their profession depends a great deal on their background, which includes their place in society, level of education, and the individual's personal drive or ambition. For example, if your character is the son of a doctor, does that motivate him to follow in his father's footsteps or to go in a completely different direction? To become a skilled craftsman did your character need a prescribed number of years of apprenticeship? Is a license or testing required for the job? What if they practiced without a license or a verifiable degree?

To help with the conflict between the characters and to move the story along it is sometimes helpful to have two opposite occupations in your main characters. Both could be in the same profession and then the conflict would be their competition for the prize, solution to a mystery, or the first to complete the quest, whatever it might be. Spencer Tracy and Katharine Hepburn in *Desk Set* were both in the business of retrieving information, she as a librarian, he an efficiency expert. Boy, did the sparks fly when they got into a competition to see who could answer the questions first.

There are also the stories in which the occupations are at different ends of the social scale. This is particularly popular in historical and Regency romances, where the duke is in love with the governess or upper-level maid but are miles apart in the strict society of the times. This is similar to a CEO falling in love with his child's teacher or the cleaning woman.

Consider the politician and the detective, the show girl and the prince, the investigative reporter and the politician, or even the cop and the school teacher. Any one of these sound familiar?

EXERCISES

- Just for fun, pick two occupations that are next to each other (see the listings on pages 150 and 151), and give them to your hero and heroine. Now, what would be their conflict?

- Now pick two occupations, one that requires a lot of schooling and one that requires no schooling. Let's say a brain surgeon and a cab driver. Or perhaps a judge and a call girl. What would be their conflict?

- Describe a profession or occupation that you are familiar with and know the inside details. How could you "create" a story around this profession or occupation?

Heroine

Character:

Profession or Occupation:

Hero

Character:

Profession or Occupation:

Villain

Character:

Profession or Occupation:

Heroine - Kayla

Kayla doesn't have a profession or job she can fall back on. She has no specific training of any kind as she never finished her Liberal Arts degree.

Why is this important?

She's trying to finish her degree via online classes and loves her latest class, the history of herbs and their uses.

Hero - Quinn

As a homicide detective, Quinn has a great respect for the law and has even considered going to night school to become a lawyer.

Why is this important?

He doesn't rush to judgment, and being in law enforcement he has the tools needed to investigate this murder.

Villain - Emily

Since Emily only works part-time, she has the time to engage in her hobbies, and flaunt her success.

Why is this important?

Being a doctor gives her the means to kill, without leaving evidence behind.

SUMMARY

By combining a character's attitude toward work with an occupation that aids the plot, you emphasize the individual's uniqueness to the story or script. Play up these attitudes and traits, especially at the beginning of your work so the reader or viewer isn't side-swiped by a talent or bit of occupation-related knowledge that seemingly comes from nowhere.

A script or copy editor would be able to identify a grammatically incorrect ransom note which in turn would give an investigator a narrower field of suspects. Secretaries are notorious for being repositories of detailed information, especially in regards to the schedule kept by the boss. Using these sorts of professional or occupational traits adds yet another layer to creating a character that lasts a long time in a reader or viewers memory.

Use this page to list your characters occupation and work ethic and explain how it will be useful in writing your story, play, or movie script.

HISTORY

OVERVIEW
Everyone is shaped by their past. Your character's history is important because it will give the reader insight into why this character thinks and acts as he or she does.

Upbringing
The early years of your character are molded by his or her place of birth, the parents' spiritual or religious beliefs, which may or may not be strongly upheld and enforced, and also by the amount and type of education the character is likely to receive.

Influences
We are all influenced by others, whether they be our parents, a relative, such as a grandmother or uncle, and by our teachers. Perhaps a grade-school teacher gave your character a failing grade which caused him to be held back a year. She received a scholarship because her high school art teacher put in a good word for her.

Successes and Regrets
He won a karate tournament in high school but never asked Gloria for a date. She danced in the holiday play, but cried when no one noticed her science project won first place.

Defining Moments
Did this character's mother die at an early age? Was he lost in a cave as a small child? Or was her twin sister murdered? Any of these events can change a person's life forever.

Time Line
This helps you keep track of the significant events in the life of your character. This can be critical if a succession of events is pivotal.

History is what makes us who we are both in real life and in our stories.

The reader needs to understand the character's background so that as the story moves along, the reader will better understand why the character is making certain choices and performing certain actions.

A word of caution: The background history of your characters should not be revealed in an "information dump." A little revelation periodically goes a long, long way.

Heroine - Kayla

Kayla was the only child in a structured middle-class family where all decisions were made by her father.

Why is this important?

Suddenly Kayla will be forced to make her own decisions and fight for an independence she has never known. She'll have to stand on her own two feet.

Hero - Quinn

He was raised by an uncaring father who beat him.

Why is this important?

Because of this abuse, he joined the army when he turned eighteen. He later went to the police academy because he wanted to be able to fight for other suffering people. He is afraid he'll be like his father so he avoids relationships.

Villain - Emily

The middle child in an upper-class family, she was always trying to get her parents' and sister's attention.

Why is this important?

Practicing medicine fed her ego. It gave her the recognition she craved as a child.

UPBRINGING

Children tend to take on the beliefs, morals, and even mimic the actions of those who raise them. Whether good or bad, the child copies what he or she sees, feels, and learns during the formative years.

The environment provided by the parents, guardian, aunt, etc., also play a part in the makeup of your character. Were they rich, dirt poor, educated, gypsies moving from town to town, or *Leave It to Beaver* parents, who were too good, too perfect, and too unreal?

Did your character grow up loved by his or her parents or was there terrible abuse in the household? Did your heroine have siblings? If so, did she get along with them or was there distrust and jealousy during her childhood years?

What about childhood friends and neighbors? Did bullies bother your character? How about the kid next door? A best friend or a competitor? Did his father scream expletives when angry? Did his mother take in the neighborhood strays? Did his dad do the cooking at home? Was her mother taking on a class-action law suit against a large company?

Education always plays a major part in any child's upbringing and this can start as early as kindergarten, although most important are the high school and college years. Did your character have a sweetheart during these early years or did she or he never date? If not, why not?

The writer should also consider the character's religious background regardless of the type, kind, and degree of spiritual training. Even if there was none, this also will define the character and his or her actions and perhaps his or her personal relationships.

EXERCISES

- This character lost her mother when she was young. Her father remarried a widow with two daughters that hate your heroine. How would this affect her life?

- His father was a coal miner. The son had aspirations of becoming a doctor, yet his family needed his small income from working in the mines to survive. How does this hero handle the situation so that it is a win-win for all concerned...or does he?

- Describe a character's up-bringing in a book or a movie that seemed very real and appealing to you. Why or how was this character's history important to the story line?

Heroine

Character:

Upbringing:

Hero

Character:

Upbringing:

Villain

Character:

Upbringing:

Heroine - Kayla

Kayla won a small scholarship because a teacher encouraged her to apply.

Why is this important?

It got her into college; showed her she could suceed on a higher academic level.

Hero - Quinn

A school psychologist showed Quinn how to channel his anger.

Why is this important?

Quinn's determination is to be different from his father. He does this by keeping his anger in check.

Villain - Emily

Emily won a four-year science scholarship.

Why is this important?

This set her on the med school path while proving her "brains" to others. It also made her the center of attention at home for a little while.

INFLUENCES

Did she have a favorite teacher in school that changed her life? Gave her a new direction or a new way to think or act?

Perhaps his Great-aunt Minnie came to visit from one of her many exciting trips and this motivated him to become an explorer, an archeologist, a deep-sea diver, or even a forest ranger.

Was his father the local preacher and because of this, he left the religious world for a time until it called him back and he, too, became a minister, but of another faith? Was the nunnery too confining for her and she needed to discover what else was outside the high walls?

Perhaps nothing motivated him. He always had it within himself. Perhaps she promised herself she would never act in a particular way, a way she loathed.

Maybe it wasn't a person, but a book or a movie that influenced your character. He saw *The Blackboard Jungle* and was determined to become a teacher. She saw *Ray* and realized that her style of piano playing could work. Watching the weekly episodes of *Law and Order* gave him the motivation to go to law school.

Or perhaps a young girl watched *Flashdance* over and over again and was determined to become a dancer. A blind person becomes inspired to write because he listens to Garrison Keeler's *Prairie Home Companion* radio show every weekend and wants to write home spun stories about his own Lake Woebegon.

Whatever the influence, good or bad, somehow it has affected your character and will show up in his or her external actions and internal beliefs.

EXERCISES

- Your hero has always looked up to his father but hated his uncle who was a drunken bum. Then suddenly he finds out the bum is actually his father. How does he handle this revelation?

- Her older brother, who had protected her all her life, has suddenly developed a serious drug habit. What should she do? Find someone to help or can she do it alone? Does she get involved in the drug scene? Brainstorm all the possible situations.

- In the last movie you liked, describe at least one influence that was important in the development of the central character. How did this influence affect the outcome of the movie?

Heroine

Character:

Influences:

Hero

Character:

Influences:

Villain

Character:

Influences:

SUCCESSES AND REGRETS

We all have regrets; whether big or little they may continue to nag at us throughout our life. Because of these poor choices we make attempts, now and then, to rectify these mistakes. These memories could be of a physical nature, an emotional event, or even a spiritual belief.

The successes might include:
- Facing challenges without losing our sense of self
- Setting and meeting a significant tough goal (finishing a novel)
- Having your first book published
- Keeping positive when diagnosed with cancer
- Finishing a painting and winning a prize or award
- Inventing a new game or designing a new software program

The regrets might include:
- Not visiting a close family member who then unexpectedly dies
- Not standing up for what is right
- Not trying to follow a deep, long-held dream
- Not finishing your book or play and then seeing almost the same story being done by someone else
- Losing a wager
- Turning down a marriage proposal

What our character thinks, does, and feels about his or her successes or regrets makes the story more interesting. Often a character has the opportunity to redeem a regret or realize that his or her presumed failure has led to disguised benefits.

These happenings can occur at any stage in life, but often have a profound affect on the rest of our lives.

Heroine - Kayla

Kayla's biggest success was finally having the courage to walk away from her husband against her parent's advice. Her biggest regret was not doing it sooner.

Why is this important?

It is a turning point in developing her independence. This gives her the courage to start to control various aspects of her life.

Hero - Quinn

Quinn's biggest success was being promoted to detective. His biggest regret was not being able to save a battered child.

Why is this important?

He wants to find the real killer because he is beginning to believe Kayla may have been falsely accused.

Villain - Emily

Emily's biggest success was going to medical school. Her biggest regret was not being able to win her parent's affection.

Why is this important?

She continually sought attention and acclaim thereby creating a perfectionist idealogy she couldn't live up to. To this day she strives for attention by being number one.

EXERCISES

- She fell for the high school "bad boy" and overlooked the nice guys. Now, fifteen years later she returns to her hometown and....

- He has lost faith in himself. Why?

- In the last movie you liked, what did the main character regret doing? How did this affect his actions later in the story?

Heroine

Character:

Successes and Regrets:

Hero

Character:

Successes and Regrets:

Villain

Character:

Successes and Regrets:

DEFINING MOMENTS

These are the pivotal points in our character's lives. An epiphany struck when he was taking a shower. Why hadn't he thought of it before? The idea was going to change his life forever.

He was well on his way to becoming a serious pianist, probably concert-hall level or featured in a world-class symphony. Then he smashed his hand in an automobile accident and his dreams were demolished.

She was an accomplished artist who suddenly went blind. Her father who taught her everything he knew about medicine and healing in a seventeenth-century world where women were not allowed to go to school, suddenly is killed and she is alone.

Defining moments could also be naturally occurring events in the history of your character, such as graduation from college, marriage, birth, or death of a child or parent, or even joining a recovery group.

These events can either be great occurrences, or in many cases they are the "bad" things that happen in life. They may be the negative happenings we all remember and wish we could go back and change.

Defining moments can also be those things we don't see coming: fired from a job he held for fourteen years; discovering she has breast cancer; losing a leg in the war; having a messy divorce; the death of a much loved pet. Any one of these can change your character's life forever.

These moments in your character's life should be used with the following page, which shows how to document them in chronological order so that when you are deep into writing the character's back story you can keep all of his or her events in the correct order.

Heroine - Kayla

When a stray dog moved into her house and her husband forced her to get rid of it... it was then that she realized she couldn't go on with her marriage.

Why is this important?

She realized she was like that stray dog — alone in her marriage and that her feelings and opinions were not important to her husband.

Hero - Quinn

The last beating his father gave him was the final straw. He knew he had to leave.

Why is this important?

Being a victim of abuse helps him to convince other victims to leave their abusive situations and try for a better life. He swears to protect the helpless.

Villain - Emily

The first time her college professor suggested she be a candidate for medical school.

Why is this important?

It gave her a specific career direction and exposed her to her medical specialty. She was recognized for her brains.

EXERCISES

- As he read the letter he realized he would have to do something drastic. What was in the letter? What did he decide to do with the information? Why?

- She was fired from her job because of something someone else did. What did that person do? How does this change her life?

- In the last movie you saw, did the main character experience an epiphany? If so, what was it? And how did this impact the plot and the character?

Heroine

Character:

Defining moments:

Hero

Character:

Defining moments:

Villain

Character:

Defining moments:

Heroine - Kayla

Kayla's time line:

- Only child - decisions made by father
- Father remarries - siblings don't like her
- Won small scholarship
- Married her husband
- Decided to leave husband against parent's advice
- Accused of husband's murder

Hero - Quinn

Quinn's time line:

- Death of his mother
- Leaving home and joining the army
- Becoming a police officer
- Unable to save a battered child
- Becoming a homicide detective

Villain - Emily

Emily's time line:

- Birthdate and her relationship in the family by order.
- Acne problems
- Scholarship
- Medical school
- Position in hospital
- First murder

TIME LINE

A time line is a quick visual guide to the significant incidents in your characters' lives.

- Did the hero get sent to juvenile hall at age eleven?
- Was she in an accident at seventeen and receive a disfiguring scar?
- Was the young girl raped by her father?

Place events such as defining moments that altered the course of your character's life on the time line. It should not only be done for both the hero and the heroine but also for the villain. You might want to highlight any place where two lives cross. Use a different highlight color if all three lives intersect. This will give you great insight to their background stories and might also provide extra motivation for their actions throughout the story. Using a time line also helps to track the actual passage of time in your story.

It is also important to determine the calendar year that your story takes place in so that you can include the various social happenings and cultural events of that specific time period. This will give the reader and the viewer an immediate sense of "being there."

General time line

Mother died Age 6	Put in jail 14	Car crash 19	Married 32	Divorced 35

Specific time line

Husband murdered 1st day	Gun found 2nd day	Fingerprints found later 2nd day	Another killing 3 days later	Hero arrested 6th day

EXERCISES

- As a child this boy first killed a raccoon in the forest near his home. After this kill, he moved to killing neighbors' pets. How does this time line prepare him for life as a killer?

- While on vacation she was in a terrible car accident, which left her with a limp. After many operations she still does not have good balance and her leg gives out every so often. How did this time line affect her life?

- She was raped in the college dorm. She is now thirty-eight and considering a serious relationship. How will a time line about this incident help the story along?

Heroine

Character:

Time line:

Hero

Character:

Time line:

Villain

Character:

Time line:

Heroine - Kayla

Since her high school days, Kayla has always second-guessed herself.

Why is this important?

It shows her indecision and insecurity. She will be forced to make decisions on her own and fight for independence.

Hero - Quinn

Quinn is extremely self-reliant as a result of his past. Raised by an abusive father and without a mother to care for him, he could only count on himself.

Why is this important?

He knows he doesn't have to rely on others and he doesn't look to others to help him. He would rather do things on his own.

Villain - Emily

Emily was influenced early on to use her mind.

Why is this important?

Winning a scholarship set her on the road to her career as a top trauma surgeon and gave her the opportunity to achieve fame. It also gave her access to drugs.

SUMMARY

Everyone has a history, including the characters we write about. By considering how our hero was raised, the individuals who influenced him, his personal successes and regrets, and pivotal moments that changed the direction of his life, you, as the author, build a multi-dimensional character.

Digging into his or her background may also provide points of conflict, internal or external, with another character.

Not all the information you gather for your character will necessarily be used. What will happen is this — you will know the individual of your story as if he or she were your best friend. If one of the characters in your story asks a question of your main character, "Why did you become a SEAL?" You, as the creator, will have the ready answer. "Because my brother was tortured and killed in a Vietnamese prison just off the coast. A SEAL would have been able to save him."

RELATIONSHIPS

STEP FOUR

OVERVIEW
Characters rarely exist alone in a story. In fact, drama, conflict, and change come about through the interaction of two or more characters. When your character discusses his life choices with his father, when he plays basketball with his buddies, when she makes love to her husband or lover, or when she goes out for a night with the girls — all these interactions help you communicate to the reader what this character is about.

Relationship with Family
Every character comes from some kind of family, whether an orphan or from a loving family. The family structure or lack of one, can make your character confident, lost, or bewildered.

Family's Background
Whatever the family background of your character, use these interactions to explain his or her instinctive reactions to love and life.

Relationship with Friends
Often a character will have a blending of family and friends. His best friend's mother may be more of a family member than his own biological mother. Emotions and connections define relationships as you create your character. All these connections should weave together to form a clear and memorable picture of your character.

Relationship with Significant Other
Defining and explaining why your character is in a relationship or searching for one will help you in clarifying who she or he is. Remember, matching your character with another in an intimate way will evoke conflict and contrast as well as harmony and love. Use the significant other in your character's life to divulge his or her most intimate thoughts, beliefs, and dreams.

Relationships have the potential to define a character more than any other aspect of their persona.

The very traits and emotions your character is weak in will be buoyed by the opposite in their significant other. Where one is emotional, the other will be logical.

Remember Agents Scully and Mulder from *The X-Files?*

Heroine - Kayla

Kayla's mother was killed when she was young. When her father remarried a woman with other children, her new stepmother made her feel left out and abandoned.

Why is this important?

She can't forgive her father for marrying this woman and allowing her new stepmother to "cut" Kayla out of his life. She dislikes the woman intensely for taking her father's undivided attention away from her.

Hero - Quinn

Quinn was raised by a drunken father who beat him. His mother died of cancer when he was young. He never had a normal childhood.

Why is this important?

Quinn has no family support system. Instead of being able to talk decisions over with an older, wiser family member, he has had to make all his decisions by himself, many of them wrong.

Villain - Emily

Emily hated her family. Being the middle child, she was constantly being compared to the other children and always fell short of the mark.

Why is this important?

Emily's resentment and jealousy festered, making her a bitter unhappy woman lacking love and support.

FAMILY

Family not only impacts your character's past history, it can also play an important role in the present and future plot points in the story. The way in which your character deals with his mother, father, siblings, and extended relatives can tell quite a bit about what makes him tick.

The very lack of family: the sudden death of the entire clan; the loss of a sibling; the desertion of a father or mother — all impact your character and help show the reader what motivates that person.

Remember, in this section we are exploring how your character interacts with her family in the present, not in the past. A family's impact can be felt throughout the story. Also consider non-family characters (those who live in the same house such as the housekeeper or nanny) who have an impact on your main character and those characters who have married into the family. Often they make wonderful villains or supportive secondary characters.

The past and present of any relationship should weave into a seamless cloth of love and hate, commitment, and obligation. Use the family, or lack of one, to help define and clarify your character's motivations, desires, and stumbling blocks.

Especially if doing a historical or family saga, you will need to keep close track of all the family, their full names, place and date of birth (and death if important to plot line), occupation and/or business location, and how your character feels about this relative. Possible issues are what your character likes best or least about the relative, what she or he wants to change in this person, and even what she or he wishes never had happened. Using the family can provide motivation and conflict in your character.

EXERCISES

- This character worshipped her mother's beauty and sophistication as a child. Now as an adult their relationship has changed. How has this change affected this character's emotional behavior?

- This character had a rocky relationship with his or her grandfather who raised him when his parents died. How does the beliefs of a different generation affect this character?

- Describe/define your character's feelings toward a pivotal family member and explain how or why this affects your character.

Heroine

Character:

Family:

Hero

Character:

Family:

Villain

Character:

Family:

FAMILY'S BACKGROUND

Families not only raise us, but they provide us with our cultural foundation. Holidays celebrated within one family may be totally unheard of in another such as Cinco de Mayo, Juneteenth, Yom Kippur, etc.

This cultural upbringing can reflect in one's attitudes and biases toward other people, groups, and individuals. For a young Hispanic male, an insult against his mother in front of him is a point of honor worth defending.

Her family came to America but refuses to learn the language. How will this affect the children? He came from a family of professionals. Both of his grandfathers, his father, and both of his uncles were doctors but he wanted to be an artist. What kinds of conflicts will this cause?

If your story is set in any time other than current history, the family background will be most important. It may influence where the family lives, whether or not they immigrate to a new land, even the relationships they are allowed to develop outside the family circle. For example, in stories set in late eighteenth and early nineteenth centuries, when divorce was still a "terrible" blow to the family, how did a woman survive the disgrace to the family? Was she forced to leave or stay and be ostracized not only by the community but also by her family?

Besides the relative's name, you might consider knowing a bit more about the people that are going to impact your character and the plot. Did they have an ancient grudge against your character? What was their status in the society of the times? And of course, how did they influence your character, either for good or evil?

Don't forget to include, if needed, influential aunts, uncles, step-parents, step-siblings, cousins, etc.

Heroine - Kayla

Kayla lost her mother when she was young. When her father remarried a woman that Kayla didn't like, she felt abandoned.

Why is this important?

Since her mother's death she has felt alone and that no one believes in her. This feeds her lack of self-confidence and the belief that she can't make it on her own.

Hero - Quinn

Quinn's family background revolved around his abusive father who never showed any affection to his son. The pair never had much in common.

Why is this important?

Quinn never had much of family life and is uneasy around families and not certain how to respond when he's shown affection.

Villain - Emily

Emily's family valued education and accomplishment. Their roots extend back to the time of the American revolution and include a famous commander.

Why is this important?

Because it adds additional pressure onto Emily to be someone of note.

EXERCISES

- This character's grandfather was denied work in NYC by English "Americans" because he was Irish. How has this trickled down to affect his current attitude?

- This character was victimized by police at the Democratic National Convention in 1968. How has this affected his daughter?

- This woman comes from a long family tradition of Naval Academy graduates. What conflicts will she generate if she chooses a different academy or career path?

Heroine

Character:

Family's background:

Hero

Character:

Family's background:

Heroine

Character:

Family's background:

Heroine - Kayla

Kayla is a shy person and never really had a best friend. However, during the course of the story, she becomes friends with Quinn.

Why is this important?

Quinn is the first man she really trusts, is open with, and feels connected to in a positive manner.

Hero - Quinn

Quinn is universally admired by his co-workers but not very friendly with them.

Why is this important?

Getting friendly means getting close. He's never been close to anyone and is afraid to love. He loved his mother and she died. He loved his father and he beat him.

Villain - Emily

Emily's only friend was another girl her age, who was her next-door neighbor during her growing-up years and who died in a car accident.

Why is this important?

Emily often wondered if they had gotten her friend to the hospital sooner, would she have lived. She becomes interested in a trauma medicine career.

FRIENDS

Companions. Buddies. Partners. The variations of friends can go from casual acquaintances who meet for breakfast every month to the person who shares every deep secret and passionate dream that can possibly be expressed.

These kinds of friends help shed light on how your lead character moves through his life, the choices he makes about how to spend his recreational time, and the way in which he interacts in a social setting.

Every choice you make about her or his friends should help you define and clarify your character. Be careful not to clutter your lead character's life with dozens of friends and acquaintances that bring nothing to the table but aimless chatter and interaction. A friend can be used to further the plot or as a sounding board for venting a problem, or planning a new adventure, and plotting a new crime.

Each friend and enemy should help you in defining your character's past and present their emotions, their thoughts, and dreams. Every friend and/or enemy in your story should have a purpose and help bring your character to life and move your story to your predetermined conclusion.

Once again your character's friends, those who are important to the story, need a full name, occupation, and most important, how that friend interacts with your characters. What does your character like about this friend? Why is she important to the story and what does your character derive from this friend?

Or does this close friend somehow become an enemy? Perhaps this friend turned enemy, lost a bet, came in second, lost his fiancée to your character, or believes a lie that has been told about him.

EXERCISES

- This character and her best friend are now in love with the same man. How does this character react in this situation? Does she break up with the man or does her friendship end with her best friend?

- This character has never had a best friend. He knows his fellow co-workers, but stays aloof and never participates in their gatherings. Why do you suppose he isn't able to make lasting and close friendships?

- Describe/define your character's emotional feelings toward his or her best friend or worst enemy and explain how important this will be in the story.

Heroine

Character:

Friends:

Hero

Character:

Friends:

Villain

Character:

Friends:

Heroine - Kayla

Kayla's husband, who she was going to leave, is suddenly killed.

Why is this important?

While sad he is dead, she is emotionally glad to be rid of him although a bit guilty of her feelings. She becomes hesitant to form any new relationships.

Hero - Quinn

Quinn is a loner who never had a loving or lasting relationship. He's only had one-night stands.

Why is this important?

This increases the conflict between himself and Kayla when he realizes the depth of his feelings for her.

Villain - Emily

She never had a boyfriend. There was always something wrong with the guys she went out with. Their flaws turned her off.

Why is this important?

A perfectionist, she knows intimate relationships can interfere in decision-making. A relationship will take the spotlight off her.

SIGNIFICANT OTHER (S.O.)

The interaction between two people can be a valuable tool for the writer in exploring the most profound layers of your characters. The way in which he feels about his wife of thirty-five years, how she chooses her next lover, the contrast between the two characters, and the detailed emotions these relationships evoke — all should give you ample ways in which to communicate your character's feelings and actions to the reader and/or viewer.

Significant others can help you drive the plot and accelerate the emotional conflict your characters experience. This relationship also highlights what your main characters want or need not only in a relationship but in life. This relationship can showcase the hero's flaw and subsequent character changes.

What needs aren't being met, both physical and emotional? What expectations does this particular significant other meet that no one else can? By using this characters relationship, whether just found, or one of long standing, you can plumb the depths of your character to show hidden passions and desires.

The significant other can also be used as a roadblock designed to stop the main character from an action for a number of reasons including fear for his or her safety, jealousy, and even self-serving motivations.

How and where they met can be used in either the back-story or it can be part of the beginning of the novel. How long have they been together? Apart? What are your character's feelings toward this person? Why did the relationship end? How did it end?

All these emotional elements can be used either to further the plot or to give more conflict to the story.

EXERCISES

- This character has just been told that her or his S.O. has been killed in an accident (car, plane, boat, etc.) or brutally murdered (shot, poisoned, etc.). What is this character's emotional reaction?

- He or she is looking for an S.O. but can't find anyone worthwhile. This character finally meets someone he or she can love, but the person is attached, engaged, or married. What is this character's reaction to the situation?

- Will the significant other be an important aspect of the story? If so, how? Describe your character's emotional feelings toward his or her significant other and explain how or why this affects your character and the story.

Heroine

Character:

Significant Other:

Hero

Character:

Significant Other:

Villain

Character:

Significant Other:

> **Heroine - Kayla**
>
> Kayla has lost her husband. Her mother is dead and she is estranged from her father and his new wife.
>
> *Why is this important?*
>
> She feels isolated and alone. Her reactions to his death are not emotional and made her appear uncaring and cold, thereby casting suspicion on her for his death.

> **Hero - Quinn**
>
> Quinn has no close friends and likes it that way. He has no family to speak of except a mean father. He has no permanent lover, only one-night stands.
>
> *Why is this important?*
>
> Quinn feels something is missing from his life but doesn't know what. Unknown to him, his one-night stands have been searches for an emotional life anchor.

> **Villain - Emily**
>
> Emily also has no one. Her sisters are married and left her. Her best friend is dead.
>
> *Why is this important?*
>
> She has no one to trust or talk to. She resents those who have the love and support of family and friends she feels she never had.

SUMMARY

Friends, family, significant others, all play important roles in a character's life. Events from past relationships influence current decisions (think of Jack Bauer in *24*). These additional characters may have a large role on screen or be part of the main character's personal history, but their influence has the ability to add to your script or story.

Think of the additional complications Mary Jane added to Spiderman's crime-fighting decisions; the guilt that weighs on a character keeping a secret (Mr. Rochester in *Jane Eyre*). Close relationships with additional characters, living or dead, can ratchet up the conflict and bring the viewer or reader more fully into the story.

PERSONALITY

OVERVIEW

Personality is a critical part of any character's makeup. It can mean the difference between a great character and a mediocre one. You know the old cliché: a villain is someone you "love to hate"? Personality is at the root of what makes the reader hate or love a character.

Think about great story characters. What was it about Scarlett O'Hara that drew us? What was special about Rhett Butler? Certainly, she was beautiful and he was a Southern hunk, but it was more than that.

Scarlett was sneaky, conniving, and manipulative, but she also demonstrated a great love for Tara and a steely determination to succeed. Add to those characteristics the fact that she was flirty and unpredictable, and she becomes a thoroughly fun character.

Rhett was considered a scalawag by some, but he was also gallant and strong in times of danger. On the other hand, he doted on his child. He changed during the course of the story from a man who didn't care what people thought to a devoted father and gentleman. Would we have loved him if he hadn't shown a softer side?

In the original *Star Trek* TV series, it was the personality of Captain James T. Kirk, Spock, and Bones, and the interplay between these men that made them so unforgettable.

As you can see on the sidebar, this section will cover various elements that make up a person's personality. Each is an important part of the character. These aspects can either help or hinder the character from achieving his or her desired goals. They determine if she will solve the mystery or he will find true love.

Finally, a part of getting to know your characters is to understand how they view their own personalities. Let your characters look into the mirror and describe themselves not only to themselves, if they can be that honest, but how they feel others think of them.

This step is about:

- traits and habits
- attitudes
- pet peeves
- strengths and weaknesses
- flaws and fears
- secrets
- beliefs
- handling a crisis
- skills and talents
- soft spot
- ambition(s)
- caring
- needs and desires
- favorites
- self-portrait

Often these elements are at the very heart of the story.

Heroine - Kayla

Kayla is quiet and generally goes along with other people's opinions. She isn't used to standing up for herself and voicing her thoughts. She bites her nails when she is nervous.

Why is this important?

She feels overwhelmed and is uncertain what to do when she is accused of killing her husband.

Hero - Quinn

He is fastidious and a loner. He doesn't drink and is an early riser. He isn't influenced by others.

Why is this important?

This maintains his focus and tunnel vision on his job and keeps him disciplined. He will go over all evidence carefully.

Villain - Emily

She is persistent and sensitive to other people but she has begun taking drugs to help with the pressure of her job.

Why is this important?

Her habit causes her to steal drugs at the hospital and she worries she will get caught. Bowing to the pressure leads to the murder of Kayla's husband.

TRAITS AND HABITS

Eye sight, intellect, curly hair, and even artistic aptitude are inherited. These qualities may even skip a generation and are called traits.

Habits are qualities which are not inherited and may include such characteristics as the character being quiet. Perhaps a character never speaks unless spoken to or never offers an opinion unless asked. Perhaps she is extremely frugal and pinches pennies. On the other hand, he is a gambler who drinks excessively. She chews her fingernails. He cheats at cards, while she habitually complains about his gaming.

To differentiate a trait from a habit, *Webster's Dictionary* states that
- a TRAIT is an "inherited characteristic" and
- a HABIT is "a behavior pattern acquired by frequent repetition."

Traits and habits help round out a person, but they also need a purpose in the story and may add to the conflict. She's a smoker who is trying to quit. She is assigned as a bodyguard to a man who loves to smoke. Think of TV's Monk. His fastidious nature might get on people's nerves, but it also suits him well as an investigator. And Columbo? His sloppiness hides a brilliant, deductive brain that suspects often disregard.

Give your character a highly visible trait or habit and a hidden trait or habit that can be used later on in the story to help "save the day."

What would be your character's most endearing habit? Or most annoying?

Which of these habits would the character like to change or eliminate all together? Could she or he do this? What conflict would this bring to the story? Remember to tie in the character's feelings and emotions to these decisions.

EXERCISES

- This character is messy. His clothes are always a bit crumpled and he needs a haircut. He falls for an excessively neat woman. How is their conflict resolved?

- This character is extremely stubborn. She meets another stubborn person. The sparks fly. How will both of them being so stubborn move the story along?

- Describe a characteristic you really liked in a recent movie. How was that trait or habit important to the story?

Heroine

Character:

Traits and Habits:

Hero

Character:

Traits and Habits:

Villain

Character:

Traits and Habits:

Heroine - Kayla

Kayla's attitude in the beginning of the story when she makes the decision to leave her husband is — "It's now or never."

Why is this important?

It provides a potential motive for murder — the desire to change her life now.

Hero - Quinn

Quinn's attitude at the beginning of the story is that Kayla is "just another name on a suspect list."

Why is this important?

He sees her as being dependent and initially not a realistic suspect.

Villain - Emily

Emily's attitude in the beginning of the story is that "I can stay in control. They will never catch me."

Why is this important?

The drugs force her to take an action she wasn't planning on.

ATTITUDES

How do you describe an attitude? The dictionary says "a mental position, feeling or emotion with regard to a fact or state."

There is more to a person than simply his no-nonsense persona. The character's attitude makes a great deal of difference in how the reader and other characters react to them. Is he funny? Arrogant? Hostile? Is she cold? Bitter? All of these attitudes can be mixed in any given character and can affect how a character approaches a problem in your story.

How would she handle an unexpected event? Would she analyze all the angles to decide how to deal with it? Or would she ignore it? Is her reaction strictly an emotional response with no thought to the eventual outcome? Why is she like this? Determining her attitude can help build an internal conflict and contribute to the final outcome of the plot. A person who is emotional will react differently than his or her logical counterpart.

Remember, the character's personality at the beginning of the story doesn't necessarily mean this character will be the same at the end of the book or script. Just as in real life, a character can and should change. He may discover cats aren't so bad, or she may re-examine her attitude regarding reporters.

Getting to know your character well will make him or her more memorable. Give your character an attitude about life in general, work, play, family, friends, and anything else you can think of. Perhaps throw in some religious, spiritual, or philosophical positions as well.

The more attitude a person has, whether great or lousy, the better your character will come across in your story. Remember this is where a great deal of emotion can be shown to the reader.

EXERCISES

- She is a highly paid, extremely driven business executive who is certain she knows exactly how to handle anything, only to find herself on a deserted island with a laid-back character who sees no reason to get back to civilization. And this leads to?

- A card shark meets a religious woman who disapproves of gambling. Together they must survive a week together in the mountains. Who changes?

- Describe an attitude that you both love and hate. How could this attitude be used in a story?

WORKSHEET

Attitudes

How does your character view work, life, or people in general? Someone who has a serious in nature is probably going to have a pretty straight-forward view of life and a no-nonsense attitude about work. Someone who is flighty or frivolous will probably be less inclined to be devoted to her job and probably has a "whatever happens, happens" philosophy about life. That character may have developed that "whatever" attitude because she views her father as a workaholic with no time for his family.

Is your character hard-boiled? A loner? Be careful in how you define attitudes. A "loner" can be viewed in different ways. Does she have a less-than-favorable attitude toward people so she stays away from them? Or is he simply shy and reluctant to interact? Either way, their attitude about the people around them will be different from characters that are naturally gregarious.

Basically, when deciding on which attitude to give to your character the writer needs to carefully consider the too much/too little aspect of the attitude.

For example, if the character needs to be brave for the story to work, how much or how little bravery does she need?

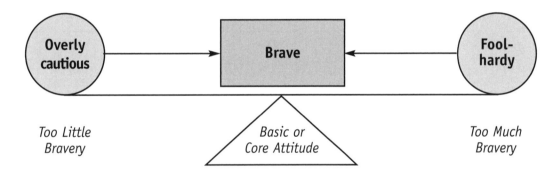

Attitudes are always a balancing act. Like the teeter-totter above, the core attitude is the middle ground while the too little and the too much sit on the far ends of the fulcrum.

What is your character's attitude when the story begins? At which end of the teeter-totter? Of course we want him to change — to move toward the middle — to become a heroic character. Let's start him out as an overly cautious individual. Some might even call him a coward. His growth or change will be how he overcomes his cautiousness.

Now, on the other hand, if our heroine is foolhardy and tries to accomplish tasks that are beyond her abilities, she will also have to change. She will have to learn how to become more cautious and reasonable.

Ah... conflict.

WORKSHEET

Attitudes

Here are a few examples of how the too much/too little process might work.

Too Little	Core Attitude	Too Much
Selfish	KIND	Sucker/pushover
Rigid	FLEXIBLE	Free-spirited
Intuitive	ANALYTICAL	Logical
Forgiving	STRICT	Judgmental

Add your own:

_____	_____	_____
_____	_____	_____
_____	_____	_____
_____	_____	_____
_____	_____	_____

There are two ways you can use this too little/too much process:

1 - give each character a different attitude and watch them change.

2 - give both characters the same attitude but at different ends of the teeter-totter. Who moves first and how much? She wants her independence, to have her own business. However, he wants a traditional family with his wife not working at an outside job and staying at home. Right away there is tension and conflict.

Heroine

Character:

Attitudes:

Hero

Character:

Attitudes:

Villain

Character:

Attitudes:

Heroine - Kayla
Kayla's pet peeve is people who allow their dogs to paw through the neighbors' trash.
Why is this important?
It shows she is meticulous when it comes to cleanliness and has pride in the appearance of her home.

Hero - Quinn
Quinn's pet peeve is people who complain about gaining weight but continually stuff themselves with junk food.
Why is this important?
He can't understand why people can't maintain discipline about something they say concerns them. He may be judgmental of Kayla's weight concerns.

Villain - Emily
Emily's pet peeve is people going into her office when she isn't there.
Why is this important?
She is private and doesn't want anyone to see the lack of personal mementos or the hidden stash of drugs.

PET PEEVES

Revealing small details about your characters also develops their personalities. Think about what they hate most, what makes their blood boil. Bad drivers? People who don't ask if others mind if they smoke? People who leave their dogs in the car without cracking open a window? The store clerk with a chip on her shoulder?

Have your character react to that pet peeve by taking either some type of external action or by having an internal emotional reaction.

What are your hot buttons? Don't be afraid to apply them to your characters. Even if it is a small mention in your story, it can go a long way toward showing who your characters are and in making them more true to life. In order for readers to relate to our stories, our heroes and heroines need to be a little like us.

No one is perfect and no one wants to read about a character with a perfect life. Remember Felix Ungar (Jack Lemmon) in *The Odd Couple* who couldn't stand a dirty dish or anything out of place? What about Jimmy the Tulip (Bruce Willis) in *The Whole Nine Yards*, who couldn't stand mayonnaise on his hamburgers?

Pet peeves vary from the tiny ones such as disliking elevator music to medium-sized ones such as cracking knuckles, phone hang-ups, leaving the cap off the toothpaste tube, sagging pants, and colorized movies to the really obnoxious ones like bad drivers who either tailgate or weave in and out of traffic hoping to gain that extra car space, unleashed dogs, and those ever-present potholes that somehow we can never avoid. Poor grammar and bad manners seem to be in a class all by themselves.

The classic female pet peeve — he left the toilet seat up!

EXERCISES

- Both of your lead characters smoke. One, however, wants to quit and is using the patch. The other one loves it too much. What kind of conflict will this lead to and how will it be resolved?

- He taps his pen continually. How do his co-workers react?

- Describe one of your pet peeves. How could it be used in a story?

Heroine

Character:

Pet peeves:

Hero

Character:

Pet peeves:

Villain

Character:

Pet peeves:

Heroine - Kayla
Kayla's strength is that she can adapt to most any situation. This has helped her up to this point in her life. Her weakness — hot fudge sundaes.
Why is this important?
She complains about her weight but makes poor food choices. She believes she can live on her own despite a lack of experience.

Hero - Quinn
Quinn's strength is that he can focus on the situation at hand and tune out distractions. His weakness — the underdog.
Why is this important?
Kayla is both a distraction and an underdog, which causes an internal conflict within Quinn.

Villain - Emily
Emily's strength is her ability to manipulate people and to hide her true self. Her weakness — drugs to calm her nerves.
Why is this important?
Her increasing dependence on drugs leads to her predicament while her ability to manipulate allows suspicion.

STRENGTHS AND WEAKNESSES

Strengths and weaknesses play an important part in making readers love or hate your characters. Put strong characters into a situation where they must conquer their weaknesses and you have a compelling story. A physically strong character who reacts quickly and decisively is commonplace, but what if he is faced with a cat-and-mouse game where taking his time and thinking through puzzles and strategies is what makes the difference? What if he has to use brain instead of brawn? His very nature calls for action, but what if he has to do the one thing he considers a weakness in others?

Have the shy computer programmer save the day by finding the magic pass code to unlock the door as the room is collapsing around her. Strengths can be more than physical or even mental. Show a character's talent for doing something unusual. Perhaps she is artistic or he has a way with children.

The secret is to define a character's strengths and weaknesses and use them in the story. Make your characters suffer and your readers will love you for it. Let the reader think the characters are facing insurmountable odds, so they can cheer when she or he finally reaches his or her goal or destination. Make your characters use or face a weakness to show real growth.

Superman is a great example. He is strong, but when near a piece of Kryptonite he loses his strength and becomes weak. Normal everyday characters sometimes have super powers when an accident occurs and they need to lift a car off of an injured loved one. Extraordinary moments and challenges force people to react in ways where they must use a strength or conquer a weakness, especially if survival is on the line.

Be sure to think through how these powers or lack of them can affect your story line.

EXERCISES

- This heroine doesn't like heights. She has to rescue the hero by climbing up a cliff. How is she going to overcome this weakness? She has to figure out a way all by herself with no help from the hero — who, by the way, is unconscious.

- Think Superman and Kryptonite. What comic strip character do you know that has super strength and a noticeable weaknesses? How does this make him more interesting?

- He loves to laugh. She doesn't find anything humorous. How will they get along?

Heroine

Character:

Strengths and Weaknesses:

Hero

Character:

Strengths and Weaknesses:

Villain

Character:

Strengths and Weaknesses:

FLAWS AND FEARS

In *Batman Begins*, a powerful inhaled hallucinogen projects an individual's private fear on the face of the person with them.

Often a character's flaws or fears drive the story. Perhaps it is a fear that needs to be overcome. Indy had to overcome his fear of snakes in the first *Indiana Jones* movie in order to save himself and the heroine. Movies that give the lead character a terrible fear of spiders and all sorts of creepy crawly things, then plunges the character into the middle of them give the reader or viewer a greater sense of fear. Remember its use in the film *Arachnophobia*? Some great fears to use include flying, snakes, spiders, heights, claustrophobia, drowning, and being buried alive. Flaws could be jealousy, envy, vanity, competitiveness, dishonesty, and greed. The list goes on and on.

Soap operas are great at using fear, such as the woman who can't go out of her house for fear of a panic attack. Or fear of germs when eating in a restaurant that finds a character wiping down the tables and utensils with antiseptic pads. Almost anything, if taken to an extreme, will work.

Flaws such as jealousy or envy are perfect for a villain and usually this flaw works to bring the villain to his or her knees and becomes his or her downfall. What about claustrophobia which was used very effectively in the movie *Panic Room*? Fear of being buried alive was used in a *CSI* segment and by Edgar Allan Poe.

Of course, the character might have one of Charlie Brown's fears. His fear of responsibility is hypengyophobia, fear of cats is ailurophobia, fear of staircases is climacophobia, or as Lucy finally says, "Do you think you might have pantophobia?" To which he replies, "Yes, that's it. Pantophobia. The fear of everything."

Heroine - Kayla

Kayla's greatest fear is that she will end up running back to her father and stepmother for financial support. Her flaw is not believing she can make it on her own.

Why is this important?

She doesn't want to revert to being taken care of by her father and living with her stepmother, a woman she dislikes, because her stepmother made her feel left out and abandoned.

Hero - Quinn

Quinn's greatest fear is that while trying to protect someone, his actions will get them hurt. His flaw — he is extremely stubborn.

Why is this important?

Quinn can't forget the death of the battered child he couldn't save and fears repeating his failure. When he finds a clue he follows it to its logical end.

Villain - Emily

Emily's greatest fear is that she will get caught. Her flaw is her arrogance.

Why is this important?

Her arrogance leads to a mistake she doesn't fix.

EXERCISES

- This heroine plays the cello. Her greatest fear is that during a concert she will either forget the music or hit a wrong note. How does she overcome her stage fright?

- He is deathly afraid of anything electric, yet he is a handyman. How will this fear cause him problems and how can he overcome his fear?

- Think about a flaw you noticed in the last movie you saw. How was this used as part of the story?

Heroine

Character:

Flaws and Fears:

Hero

Character:

Flaws and Fears:

Villain

Character:

Flaws and Fears:

Heroine - Kayla

Kayla is writing a novel — a romance.

Why is this important?

She is not good at expressing herself and her opinion to other people but she finds it easy and fun to do on paper.

Hero - Quinn

Quinn keeps his childhood and his beatings a secret.

Why is this important?

In order for Quinn and Kayla to become close and fall in love, he must tell her his secret.

Villain - Emily

Emily's biggest secret is that of being a murderer.

Why is this important?

If her secret is revealed, she'll go to prison.

SECRETS

Secrets can play a big role in how your characters deal with the challenge ahead and with their conflicts. Will the secret be important enough to cause conflict? Why is the character hiding the secret? What will be lost if the secret becomes known?

In the movie *Sleeping with the Enemy*, the audience knows why Julia Roberts is skittish about starting a new relationship, but her new friend Ben can't quite figure out the problem and this secret adds to the conflict in their relationship. Ilsa, in *Casablanca*, kept a big secret from Rick and it was what eventually pulled them apart in Paris. When she finally admits the truth it sets up his grand gesture at the end of the movie and gives them both back what they had shared many years before.

Secrets can be large or small. They can be something as simple as a toupee or as large as having committed a murder in the past. William H. Macy in *Fargo* secretly arranged to have his wife kidnapped, while Obi Wan and Yoda kept the identity of Luke's father and the existence of his sister secret from him in the *Star Wars* sagas.

Secrets are one way of building the internal struggle that each main character has to resolve as well as building empathy with the intended audience. Secrets can be about almost anything. She has a sexy tattoo on her butt. He is a closet homosexual. She had not only one affair while married, but several. He killed his father when he was young when he caught him beating his mother.

Villains are perfect characters to harbor secrets for many of these unspoken events will have shaped the bad guy into what he is today. Heroes and heroines need their secrets, too. It is often the unveiling of these secrets that helps the character grow and change into a better person.

EXERCISES

- He'd been convicted of a crime he did not commit so he fakes his own death. How does he deal with the knowledge that someone has found out what he has done?

- She was not attractive, so she had plastic surgery and changed herself into a new person. Will she reveal her secret to the man who proposed to her?

- She worked in a strip club as an exotic dancer. Why does she want to keep her past occupation under wraps now?

Heroine

Character:

Secrets:

Hero

Character:

Secrets:

Villain

Character:

Secrets:

Heroine - Kayla

Kayla believes that exercise and diet can help her self image. She also believes all life should be treated with respect.

Why is this important?

She knows that eating properly and exercise are good for her but she loves junk food and finds it hard to resist. She also stops a stray dog from being beaten.

Hero - Quinn

Quinn has a strong belief in justice. He believes in giving the underdog a fighting chance, but at the same time he has a strong sense of right and wrong.

Why is this important?

His initial reaction to Kayla is to believe she is guilty, but her protestations of innocence touch him and he questions his sense of what is right and wrong.

Villain - Emily

Emily grew up in a devout Catholic family where there is a strong emphasis on sin and redemption and valuing all human life.

Why is this important?

Emily carries a heavy burden of guilt for the murder of Kayla's husband and the subsequent murders she commits.

BELIEFS

Whether spiritual, religious, political, or those learned from your parents, strong beliefs can steer your character into unthinkable actions a more moderate person would never consider. The unshakable belief that a certain person lied or betrayed someone can also cause a reaction on the part of your character.

She may decide to do humanitarian work in Africa because her religious beliefs ask for a year of work in a mission area. He may go to India to seek further enlightenment on how to live more harmoniously. He may make a pilgrimage to the Holy Lands of his faith, stepping far beyond his comfort zone.

Beliefs can be as simple as believing in family, hearth, and home. A character can believe in justice and freedom. A character can be paranoid and believe everyone is out to get him. A character can believe she will never fall in love. A character can believe in an eye for an eye.

A young person's beliefs are usually quite different from an adult's beliefs as they are more centered around just themselves, such as "What is mine is mine," "Mom is always right," to "There is a monster under the bed," while an adult's beliefs might include not only his whole family, but his community, the planet, and perhaps even the universe. These beliefs could be anything from "All people are greedy," "All men want is sex," "All women want is money," to "The police and governments are corrupt" to "Flying saucers."

In *Gone With the Wind*, part of Scarlett's life revolved around her mistaken belief that she was in love with Ashley Wilkes. Because of this the course of her life was changed in many ways. At the end, when she finally realizes that she was wrong in that belief, her final confrontation with Rhett is set into motion.

EXERCISES

- He's been deeply religious all his life. He falls in love with a nonbeliever. How do they work out their differences?

- She's worked in the woman's movement and is a strong advocate of the right of each woman to have total control of her own body. He doesn't. Put the situation in any historical reference and what will happen?

- He believes most law enforcement personnel are corrupt. She is a politician. What happens next?

Heroine

Character:

Beliefs:

Hero

Character:

Beliefs:

Villain

Character:

Beliefs:

Heroine - Kayla

Kayla hates confrontation and avoids it if at all possible.

Why is this important?

She will have to learn to face her conflicts and crisis that turn her life upside down. She'll confront Emily as she becomes more self-assured.

Hero - Quinn

Quinn is good at handling a major crisis. He's a level-headed, coolly rational person.

Why is this important?

Give him a minor crisis, like a crying baby and he has trouble knowing what to do. This demonstrates how good he is with things that don't touch him personally, while he lacks the importance of affection and closeness.

Villain - Emily

Emily stays externally calm while maintaining her perfectionist standards during a crisis.

Why is this important?

Her calm during emergencies has developed a confident decision maker in the emergency room.

HANDLING A CRISIS

How a character handles a crisis can provide a visual demonstration of your character's strengths and weaknesses.

Does your character faint at the sight of blood? Does a shy woman become a warrior when medical treatment is denied her lover? Does he scream at little things but stay surprisingly calm during a major crisis? Does she contain her emotions in public only to cry hysterically in private?

How many ways can you show your heroine's strengths and good judgment with a major crisis at work and then come home to fall apart over a small household emergency? Or what about the person who handles a small crisis well, but then falls apart when the big emergency occurs?

The crisis could be a simple paper cut, fixing a flat tire, having a bad hair day, taking any type of a certification test (such as the bar exam), or getting a "Dear John" letter. Other problems that require handling and "test" your character might be moving to a foreign country, getting a divorce, surviving a flood, earthquake, fire, or hurricane.

This is useful not only for your hero or heroine, but it could say a lot about the villain as well. Think about having a meek person suddenly becoming a leader when the chips are down, or a leader falling apart when he is needed most. Showing how characters respond to a crisis will make their handling of the final conflict more believable.

Think of all the action movies you have seen when a crisis looms and there doesn't seem to be any solution to the problem when one of the secondary characters suddenly comes up with an idea or a tool that the hero or heroine can use to save the day.

EXERCISES

- He's been responsible for the implementation of a new software program designed to protect client confidentiality only to find the system was hacked into the first day. How does he react?

- She's worked her entire life for a major auto company. Now it's being downsized and her position eliminated with the offer of early retirement. How does she react?

- How do you react to the minor and major crises that come your way? Choose one to write about. Draw from your memory the emotions you experienced.

Heroine

Character:

Handling a crisis:

Hero

Character:

Handling a crisis:

Villain

Character:

Handling a crisis:

Heroine - Kayla

Kayla is a very good cook.

Why is this important?

Her cooking skills will help her start a catering business.

Hero - Quinn

Quinn is well known for his skill in solving puzzles and being able to think through investigations to a logical conclusion. He is also an able marksman. In his spare time he is a skilled wood carver.

Why is this important?

His skills as an investigator help with his work, while his talent in woodworking helps him relax on the weekends.

Villain - Emily

Emily is not only a skilled surgeon but she is skilled in suturing.

Why is this important?

She has always been self-conscious of her scars and wants to prevent that trauma for her patients.

SKILLS AND TALENTS

A character's skills and talents should play a role in the story you are telling. Maybe your heroine works as a police officer and comes home to play beautiful love songs on the piano as a way of relaxing.

In *Jurassic Park*, Lex was teased by her brother because she was bad at climbing trees, but she saved the day by getting all the park functions back online because of her computer skills.

Perhaps your heroine, who is average looking and a bit on the shy side plays the guitar or is an excellent swimmer or tennis player. He is a computer nerd who in his free time takes up ballroom dancing and becomes a marvelous flamenco dancer.

She is a talented painter, yet doesn't have any social skills. He is a stand-up comedian, but is afraid of talking to women. He is an expert piano player but can't read music or perhaps an excellent mechanic who never learned how to drive a car. She is an outgoing speaker but has poor reading skills or perhaps a successful party planner who is afraid of crowds.

Gourmet cooks are great fun to use especially in romances, however, there have been great murder-mysteries written about murdering cooks.

Skills in the area of computers now play an important role especially for the secondary characters in many of the high-tech action movies where the hero or heroine needs information but only the computer expert can find or retrieve it from an encrypted or hidden file.

Skills and talents enhance a story or script and reveal more about what makes your character memorable.

EXERCISES

- He's a talented chef at home, but a hard-edged CEO at work. How does his skill shine in public?

- She's worked hard to get the failing company out of junk bond status. How does she apply this skill to her religious beliefs?

- She is a literature professor at an Ivy League school who writes steamy romances in her spare time under another name. What happens when the school finds out about her writing talents?

Heroine

Character:

Skills and Talents:

Hero

Character:

Skills and Talents:

Villain

Character:

Skills and Talents:

Heroine - Kayla
Kayla has a soft spot for animals.
Why is this important?
She gives into her feelings and gets a puppy. She prevents a neighbor from hurting a dog.

Hero - Quinn
Quinn has a soft spot for abused kids.
Why is this important?
He volunteers at a local shelter for abused and neglected children. He relates well to children.

Villain - Emily
Emily has a soft spot for patients who are terminal.
Why is this important?
She kills the terminal patients so they won't suffer after they leave the hospital.

SOFT SPOT

The soft spot is also called a "blind spot." This is where the loving mother knows her child could *never* do anything wrong. It may also be the tyrant who knows his daughter will never do anything right.

Maybe strays are his soft spot and he now has a house full of abandoned cats. He is the doctor who has a soft spot for people who don't have adequate health care. What about the lawyer who does pro-bono work or the attorney in the public defender's office who won't quit because she has a soft spot for the people she defends?

Your character's soft spot "humanizes" the hero or heroine, despite obvious flaws, to become someone the reader relates to. It is also interesting to give the villain a soft spot of some kind. Perhaps the killer is kind to small babies or gives money to the homeless. Remember, a villain is more believable if she or he isn't totally evil; even Hannibal Lector had a soft spot for Clarice.

Not all characters, of course, need a soft spot, but if your main character is hard edged with a definite attitude, perhaps giving him or her some type of a soft spot will help with the transition that will be necessary in order for the character to grow and become a "better" person.

Frank (Jason Stratham) in *The Transporter 2* develops a soft spot for a child who is then kidnapped. Often in Regency stories, the hero who is a "man-about-town" with a soft spot for children, and this proves to the heroine that he really is an honorable man whom she would love to marry.

Maybe your two main characters are drawn together because they both love old movies or they both volunteer and work with the elderly in the same nursing home. When your two main characters have the same soft spot this can be an interesting way to bring them together.

EXERCISES

- He has owned a small cafe for several years and has a soft spot for kids who come around asking for food but can't pay. How does he react when a kid breaks into his place to steal food?

- She's a social worker and has a blind spot where the most troubled kids are concerned. How does she react when one of the kids she is trying to help is implicated in a murder?

- How does a single mother react when she discovers that her "perfect" daughter was caught shoplifting?

Heroine

Character:

Soft spot:

Hero

Character:

Soft spot:

Villain

Character:

Soft spot:

Heroine - Kayla
Kayla longs to be both financially and emotionally independent, first from her father and then from her husband.
Why is this important?
This will aid her when she works to clear herself of the murder charge.

Hero - Quinn
Quinn is happy where he is and has no ambition to try to become Chief of Police. He is more interested in simply getting the job done and upholding justice.
Why is this important?
Part of his ambition is to accomplish what he sets out to do. That includes arresting guilty people, which he believes Kayla to be.

Villain - Emily
Emily wanted to be a concert pianist.
Why is this important?
She was self-conscious about playing in front of a large group of people and going on tour.

AMBITION(S)

Ambition or even a lack of it can be very helpful when defining your characters. Someone who is driven to succeed can be ready to do anything to get to the top. In *Working Girl*, Sigourney Weaver's character (Katherine Parker) is filled with ambition, but so is Tess McGill. Tess's ambition is held back by her tyrannical boss, but she finally gets the opportunity to show what she can do. Both characters have the driving ambition to succeed in the corporate world, though they go about it in different ways. Tess works hard, while Katherine cheats.

Contrast Tess's or Katherine's drive with that of a character like Jack (Michael Douglas) in *Romancing the Stone*; Jack's ambition is to earn enough money to buy a sailboat so he can remain free to do as he pleases.

Ambitions go a long way toward honing our skills and talents. A character may decide the path her life takes is based on the strength of her commitment to her dream. If she developed a sense of right and wrong at a young age, she may feel the ambition to be a judge and sentence "bad" people, thus sending the character to college, law school, and into the legal system. Is her ambition so great she shuns relationships? What will happen when she meets a man who will only "have" her if she gives up her dream? Will she wait for a man who will allow her to continue with her ambitions?

Ambitions can be the source of a character's internal drive or the motivation for his or her action or the internal conflict that causes a character to behave in a certain way. In general, ambitions can fuel the plot dramatically.

Certainly villains have ambitions. Maybe it's to steal more money, to have more power, to rule a bigger kingdom, or even to put a virus in all the world's computers. Remember, a villain doesn't see their ambitions in a negative light.

EXERCISES

- He's been a fireman for ten years but wants to change careers as his ambition is to become a chef. How will his family react?

- She's worked as a real estate agent for years, but wants to start her own lingerie design business. How will she justify the sudden change in career when she is a single mother with two kids to support and an ex-husband threatening to sue for custody?

- He is the CEO of a large company. Suddenly he decides to build his own sailboat and sail around the world. How will he justify his actions to his partners?

Heroine

Character:

Ambition(s):

Hero

Character:

Ambition(s):

Villain

Character:

Ambition(s):

Heroine - Kayla
Kayla cares about losing weight and getting healthy.
Why is this important?
She can't stop eating junk food.

Hero - Quinn
Quinn cares about abused children.
Why is this important?
When a child tries to bond with him, he won't allow himself to become emotionally involved.

Villain - Emily
Emily cares about her reputation.
Why is this important?
She is meticulous in her work. When a mistake in surgery causes someone to die, she covers up the death so her reputation stays intact.

CARING

The writer can use "caring" to help build conflict in a story. When one character cares greatly about something, he will have a great conflict with anyone who does not share this passion.

Here are a few examples:

- The cop who believes in honesty loves a woman who tells social white lies.
- The tree-hugger who wants to preserve the forest fights with a logger who is selling the lumber.
- The antique dealer meets an artist who "copies" masterpieces.
- The mother who loves her son so much she sabotages all of his romantic relationships.
- A historian who cares about antiques and how to separate the real from the fake but is arrogant and condescending to people who aren't as knowledgeable.

When you give any one of your main characters a cause they truly believe in, the story and conflict that follows is much easier to write. This is part of the strength of the character.

Once again, it is important to note that this aspect of a personality doesn't have to be a big element in the character's life. Little acts of caring simply make the character more human. Your heroine cares that her bedroom is neat, while the hero only cares about having the nicest lawn on the block. Perhaps she cares about helping the homeless, the less fortunate, or desperately ill children, and then becomes a social worker. Maybe he cares about having enough money for a rainy day and so becomes a miser. What about the grandmother who simply cares for her grandchildren and takes over raising them when her only daughter becomes a drug addict?

EXERCISES

- He is in politics and as mayor he cares for all the citizens. However his lover cares only for making money through shady "deals." How is this conflict resolved?

- She's worked for an advertising company and cares more about the company than the owner. How will she react when the company faces a hostile takeover?

- How do two people who claim to have a child's best interest at heart react when the court finds them unfit parents?

Heroine

Character:

Cares about:

Hero

Character:

Cares about:

Villain

Character:

Cares about:

Heroine - Kayla

Kayla wants a puppy very badly.

Why is this important?

She needs to care for something. The puppy fills a lonely empty space inside her.

Hero - Quinn

Quinn needs to help people.

Why is this important?

Because no one was there to help him when he was growing up.

Villain - Emily

Emily needs to be in control.

Why is this important?

She does this to cover up not only her medical mistakes but she believes she is helping these people by ending their suffering. Being in control reduces mistakes and helps her maintain her professional reputation.

NEEDS AND DESIRES

Does your character really "need" a new job, more money, a new watch, or does he just "desire" this?

What is the difference between a need and a desire?

- A **need** is a lack of something desirable or useful
- A **desire** is a longing or wish for something that may or may not be attainable

Does she need a companion, someone to talk to so she won't feel alone in the world, or does she desire a mate, someone to cater to her every whim? Does she need a new piece of jewelry or is she just trying to impress her neighbor? Does she need a new pair of shoes or does she desire them because they are the latest style?

He desires to be macho so he exercises every day at the gym. He desires a new car, but is poor so he steals one. She desires to lose weight but needs to eat desserts because they fill an empty, emotional space inside her.

Harry Potter **needs** friends and a sense of belonging.

Rose in *Titanic* **desires** an opportunity to experience a life without social restrictions.

People need love and in turn this gives them the desire to raise a family. Villains may desire revenge as they need their enemies to suffer.

We all desire excellent health and a perfect body, but what we need is good food, exercise, and a good genetic background for this to become a reality. Need and desire often go hand in hand with each other.

EXERCISES

- Her husband divorced her for a younger woman. What does she need in order to get her life on track?

- His brother achieved financial success. What does this younger sibling desire that his elder brother has?

- She is a twin, but she needs to feel special. How does she do this?

Heroine

Character:

Needs and Desires:

Hero

Character:

Needs and Desires:

Villain

Character:

Needs and Desires:

Heroine - Kayla
Kayla was never the favorite child in her family after her father remarried.
Why is this important?
She wants to be the favorite of someone and it drove her to marry a man who wasn't right for her.

Hero - Quinn
Quinn has a favorite shirt he likes to wear.
Why is this important?
His only favorite object is transitory. He doesn't want to be attached to anything. However he does keep a small picture of his mother in his desk drawer.

Villain - Emily
Emily has a favorite pair of shoes she wears in the operating room.
Why is this important?
They keep her feet supported so they don't ache after long hours of standing. She considers them essential to her operating success and gets nervous when they disappear.

FAVORITES

What your character selects as a favorite can define who that character is and make a difference in how they function. Going to a favorite bar or having a favorite drink or food makes a character seem like a real person.

The women of *Sex and the City* loved clothes and fashion. Carrie Bradshaw had a whole closet of her favorite items — shoes — and she spent a good portion of her salary on them. Tom Cruise as Navy lawyer Lt. J.G. Daniel Kaffee in *A Few Good Men* had a favorite bat he needed to keep handy, and he said he always thought better with it in his hands. Shirley in *Laverne and Shirley* had a Boo-Boo kitty from her childhood.

These elements give your characters a particular "feel" and make them different from other people. You can always use the favorite item in a story, whether it is the villain destroying a cherished keepsake so your character goes after him or a favorite restaurant burning down and your character wanting to help rebuild it.

In many stories, there is a favorite spot to which a character goes to simply think or reflect on her life. She may even bring her lover to this special place.

For women, a favorite object is usually a piece of jewelry, a memento, or even their pet. For men, cars rank high on the list as do sports items and, of course, a pet. But almost anything will work. A favorite could simply be a poster, a favorite CD, or a personal diary.

For a skier, winter might be a favorite season. A painter might have a special color; a musician, a special song.

Think of the things you love and use them in your novel.

EXERCISES

- He's been going to the same coffee shop for years and has made friends with the owner. He went to this shop because he felt lonely. What will he do now that his favorite place is closing?

- She's worked in a library for several years and her position has changed over the years. Finally she has found her favorite job, cataloging new books. Now she is being moved to her least favorite position, the checkout desk. Use this to create a scene for your story.

- Joe's lucky baseball bat is missing. Because of this he strikes out in the bottom of the ninth. Write a scene depicting his emotions.

Heroine

Character:

Favorites:

Hero

Character:

Favorites:

Villain

Character:

Favorites:

Heroine - Kayla
Kayla sees herself as plump with unmanageable hair.
Why is this important?
Her interpretation of her outward characteristics reflect her lack of self-confidence.

Hero - Quinn
Quinn sees himself as a take-charge, detail-oriented cop who never gets emotionally involved.
Why is this important?
He changes enough to risk an emotional attachment and loosens his reins of control.

Villain - Emily
Emily sees herself as being in total control despite her drug addiction.
Why is this important?
It leads to over-confidence and her downfall.

SELF-PORTRAIT

How a character views her or himself at the beginning of the book or movie may be another good way to show who the character is and provide part of the conflict for your story. The character who has great inner confidence is totally different from the character who views himself as a loser. The first carries himself with supreme confidence, while the second might shuffle around hoping no one notices him.

Remember the movie *The Picture of Dorian Gray* and how the portrait ages? In *The Shipping News*, think about Kevin Spacey's character, both in the beginning of the movie and at the end. Think about how the character of Joan Wilder grows and changes during *Romancing the Stone*.

Rick Blaine from *Casablanca* is very confident at the start of the movie, but by the middle he is mentally wounded and by the end cautious about life. Tess McGill from *Working Girl* puts herself "down" when the action starts but soon moves to being bold and by the end of the movie is confident in her actions. Han Solo from *Star Wars* is self-centered at first, then becomes concerned, and by the end of the story is altruistic.

To apply this to your characters, think of how a character with supreme confidence might react when he runs across something or someone that he can't control.

What if a character has something at stake that she values so highly, like the life of a loved one, that she has to rise above her "loser" tag and be someone heroic? How will she view herself at the end if she pulls it off? A confident character might be a little different when she or he realizes not everything comes easily or if a hasty decision has disastrous consequences.

EXERCISES

- He's been a football jock all his life and plans on being drafted by the NFL. He shatters his leg skiing. How does he look at himself now?

- She's worked hard to overcome a persistent weight problem she had as a teen. Now, she's going to her ten-year high school reunion. How does she look at herself?

- How do you view yourself?

Heroine

Character:

Self-portrait:

Hero

Character:

Self-portrait:

Villain

Character:

Self-portrait:

Heroine - Kayla

Kayla is a shy woman who sees herself as overweight with terrible hair. She has low self-esteem and avoids confrontations. She longs to be independent from her father and her husband.

Why is this important?

After being charged with murder she will be forced to change the way she sees herself by finding an inner strength.

Hero - Quinn

Quinn is a take-charge loner who is adept at handling a crisis.

Why is this important?

He doesn't let himself get close to anyone.

Villain - Emily

Emily's confidence and need to be in control begin to disintegrate.

Why is this important?

It reveals a series of mistakes showing she is not in total control.

SUMMARY

Personality is a vital part of who your characters are and how they react to the people and situations around them. Take time to get to know all of the various elements of their personalities remembering that not all people have all the elements listed in this section.

Many of the sections covered in this step define intangible qualities that you have created for your character. Habits, attitudes, and favorite belongings provide a colorful layer of personality that will affect his or her actions further down the story's path.

Thoroughly knowing the personalities of the major players gives the author confidence in determining the choices characters make. We know Sherlock Holmes will handle a crisis in a different manner than John McClane from the *Die Hard* movies, yet both are heroic.

BODY LANGUAGE AND SPEECH

STEP SIX

OVERVIEW

How we walk and talk tells the world a great deal about who we are and how we perceive ourselves. Whether it's Eliza Doolittle saying *"Just you wait 'enry 'iggins, just you wait,"* or the Professor Higgins saying *"Women are irrational...they're nothing but exasperating, irritating, vacillating, calculating, agitating, maddening, and infuriating hags!"* we immediately know who comes from the lower dregs of society and who comes from the English upper crust.

Body Language

Your hero stands stoically at the window, staring into space, hands fisted at his side, silent as a tomb. In the context of your story, your reader knows exactly what he is communicating without him having to utter a word. While not a character trait in and of itself, body language does reveal a character's inner emotions and moods. In the above example, it is easy to see that this individual is unhappy. Perhaps he has just learned of a betrayal and is processing the ramifications, trying his utmost to keep his temper in check. If you've done your job as the author, we know if this hero has a problem with anger, patience, or is easily frustrated.

Speech

How your characters use speech patterns can go a long way toward not only defining who they are in the story but where they come from. Characters don't necessarily have to change during the course of the story, but it can happen. Your southern gentleman wouldn't lose his twang, although a hardened character who curses frequently may have toned down his language by the end if the story involved his having to care for a bunch of nieces and nephews.

Identifying Tags

Tags are those special action or verbal phrases that the reader comes to identify with certain characters.

Here are a few movies that use speech and body language to the fullest:

Hang 'Em High
The Outlaw Josey Wales
The Terminator
Gone With the Wind
Escape from New York
Gypsy
The Sound of Music
Cool Hand Luke
Now, Voyager
Traffic
Freejack

Heroine - Kayla
Kayla has a tendency to fidget when faced with controversy.
Why is this important?
Initially it gives the impression she has something to hide. As she grows in confidence she won't feel the need to fidget.

Hero - Quinn
Quinn maintains a sturdy stance. His eyes are steady and never look away when he talks to someone.
Why is this important?
His unwavering gaze makes the guilty nervous.

Villain - Emily
Emily has a light, graceful step. She is very poised and calm.
Why is this important?
Her body language deflects initial suspicion away from her.

Body Language

Some researchers report that almost 50 percent of our communication is based on body language. What are some of the basics of body language? Facial expression, body stance, positioning of our hands, and the movements of our arms are all forms of body language. These are signals we use and interpret so often it has become second nature to us. We need to remember to give our characters the same intuitive abilities.

Often we think of this tool as sending negative signals, but body language may reveal positive messages (thumbs up). Another example is arms-crossed. On the surface, this would indicate a "stay-away-from-me" protective stance, but if your character is shy, nervous, or uncomfortable in his or her dress or situation, those arms might not be foreboding but an indication of nervousness.

How close do your two characters stand to one another? Does one point or wag a finger while talking? How about flaring nostrils, twitching or shifting eye(s), closed eyes, the rolling of the eyes upward, or the constant pushing of glasses back up on the nose. Feet also can be used: Kicking the ground, shifting from one foot to the other, or even rocking back and forth is part of body language. What does playing with the hair mean? Lots of heroes, when frustrated, often "run their fingers through their hair."

Don't forget the hands. The chewing of fingernails, the clasped hands either in the lap or behind the back, clenched fists, or hands bowed in submission or steepled as in prayer can give a subtle message.

Remember, too, body language often reveals the real meaning of the words being spoken. A clenched fist, if accompanied by a smile and loud cheers, indicates happiness as opposed to anger.

EXERCISES

- This character is extremely shy. He holds his head down, doesn't make eye contact, etc. How would this affect his ability to get a date? Or a job?

- She's nervous. Clasps and unclasps her hands. Crosses and uncrosses her legs. Twists in her seat, consistently trying to find a more comfortable position. How would she sit if she wasn't nervous?

- Describe a character in a movie you have just seen that used body language to help you, the viewer, better understand the situation. Why was this body language important to the story?

Heroine

Character:

Body language:

Hero

Character:

Body language:

Villain

Character:

Body language:

SPEECH

"I'll be baacck."	"Bullshit!"
"A Jedi you will be."	"You don't say?"
"To be or not to be."	"Darlin'."

Speech and speech patterns are yet another way you can give the reader more information about your characters.

Some of the aspects of speech that can be used to vary it include: tone, inflection, pitch, quality, rate, accent, education, place in society, age, vocabulary, and, of course, sex. For example, the tone of one's speech could be playful, angry, serious, or even teasing. The inflection could be singsong or a monotone. Pitch would be high, low, nasal, soft, loud, or deep. The quality could be careful, sophisticated, or squeaky. The character could slur his words.

Is your main character a pre-school teacher? If so, she is likely to use simple words. A former football star? He may use analogies (comparisons) that are laden with sports references. These patterns show up in the course of regular speech. Don't go out of your way to add them, but if your football player has to explain something, remember to think as he does. Make sure the metaphors and similes go with the personality you've developed.

Speech can also be used to identify your character. What would Jessica Tandy's Daisy in *Driving Miss Daisy* be without her southern accent? A teen, however, needs to use a favorite slang word on occasion.

Here we must insert a word of caution. Speech accents are to be used like seasoning — sparingly. If your character stutters, it is not necessary to show the stuttering every single time a real person would stutter. Readers will automatically associate a stuttering pattern with that character.

Heroine - Kayla

Kayla prattles on when she's upset or when she is trying to soothe someone's anger or disappointment.

Why is this important?

She is uncomfortable in emotional situations and feels a need to "cloak" the silence with chatter.

Hero - Quinn

Quinn is a man of few words. His speech is clipped and to the point.

Why is this important?

He's direct and to the point and this bothers many people.

Villain - Emily

Emily is very soft spoken and highly educated.

Why is this important?

Inside she is seething, while outwardly she controls her temper. She makes fun of others with words she knows they don't understand.

EXERCISES

- She stuttered as a child. She worked hard and now has perfect speech, except when she is angry. How could this be used effectively in a story? (Stuttering Stanley from *The Sixth Sense*)

- His accent was interesting / annoying / hard to understand / soothing / highly educated / barely recognizable as English / full of swear words / slurred, etc. Make up a couple of lines of pure dialogue that show these variables.

- In the last movie you saw, describe the speech of the character you liked best. Why do you think his or her speech affected you so? What were their pet phrases?

Heroine

Character:

Speech:

Hero

Character:

Speech:

Villain

Character:

Speech:

Heroine - Kayla

Kayla's favorite expression is *"You don't know the half of it."*

Why is this important?

It reflects Kayla's quiet gentle personality and indicates she doesn't tell everything.

Hero - Quinn

"Fubar."

Why is this important?

Because he sees most situations through his military and police training and fubar means *"F***ed Up Beyond All Repair."*

Villain - Emily

"Don't worry. You're in good hands."

Why is this important?

It is supposed to inspire confidence, but when uttered by Emily, it is tainted with a darker, deadlier meaning only the reader and Emily know.

IDENTIFYING TAGS

A tag is a special quirk given to a character as a way of setting that individual apart. It might be an expression such as *"Bloody hell"* that only a British nobleman uses. The tag might be a twitch of the eye or the nose.

Does she have a particular substitute for swear words such as *"Rats,"* which would indicate to the reader who she is? Does he snap his finger at the end of a command?

Usually it is not wise to give two characters the same tag or you will confuse the reader. Notable exceptions are:

- *The Kid* with Bruce Willis and Spencer Breslin, wherein both adult and child do exactly the same things.
- *Twins* with Arnold Schwarzenegger and Danny DeVito wherein each twin, although they don't look alike, has the exact same habit.
- *The Spy Who Shagged Me* with Mike Myers and Verne Troyer as Austin Powers and his clone Mini-me. They have the same habit of pressing the back of their pinkie to their lips.

A few more tags are:

- Chewing a pencil, toothpick, or pipe
- Clearing the throat
- Playing with jewelry, either a necklace or perhaps a ring
- Cracking knuckles
- Playing with a paper clip

And the list goes on. What are some of your favorites?

EXERCISES

- A man compulsively chews the ends of his pens. How can this tag be used effectively in a story?

- A woman twists her hair when she is nervous because it helps to calm her. How can this be used in a story?

- His favorite pastime while on the phone is doodling. Does he draw geometric designs or cartoons? What does this mean?

Heroine

Character:

Identifying tags:

Hero

Character:

Identifying tags:

Villain

Character:

Identifying tags:

Heroine - Kayla

Kayla is nervous in emotional situations, which cause her to fidget and become quite chatty.

Why is this important?

Her talkativeness and fidgeting cast suspicion on her while she was at her dead husband's side.

Hero - Quinn

Quinn has an unwavering gaze and uses direct language that makes the guilty quite nervous.

Why is this important?

This intimidates most people, making him an imposing figure, as well as keeping intimate relationships from developing.

Villain - Emily

Emily is poised with a cool, collected, and calm persona.

Why is this important?

Because it hides the drug-addicted killer within.

SUMMARY

The use of body language, speech, and identifying tags help relate more about the personality of your characters to the reader.

Body language clues let the reader know if a character is lying, nervous, confident, or putting up a good front. They have the potential to reveal internal feelings without spoken words. Seasoned directors coax these emotions from their actors and by doing so evoke stellar performances.

Speech patterns play a role as well. From regional drawls to a rapid fire interrogation the reader and viewer learn more about a character's emotional state.

Finally, tags such as a limp, eye patch, left-handedness, and even an alcohol preference (James Bond's martinis are "Shaken, not stirred") help set your characters apart and make them live on in the minds of others.

WARDROBE AND POSSESSIONS

STEP SEVEN

OVERVIEW
It's time to dress your character and give him or her some possessions to reflect who that person is.

Wardrobe
What he or she wears gives the reader insight into who they are. Perhaps it's just as important what your character doesn't wear. No watch. No rings, no bracelet or necktie. The character is perhaps not bothered by society's time-oriented meetings or making splashy impressions. Lots of jewelry, however, might mean that the character has a self-esteem problem.

Grooming
From overly sweet scents to smelly body odor, how a person preens gives the reader even more insight into their persona.

Vehicle
Does he drive a sports car, a ten-speed bike, a pickup truck, or a Harley Davidson? Each vehicle brings to mind a certain kind of person and gives the reader added knowledge of the character.

Pets
Does she keep a cat or a bird? Is he a dog lover or does he raise exotic animals? Not keeping a pet also says a lot about the character.

Most prized possession
Everyone has something that they prize and would be heartbroken if it was stolen, lost, or burned beyond recognition. It could be a necklace that her late mother gave her, or a heavy gold ring that was handed down from generation to generation. Perhaps it is simply a picture of a dead child or a Shelby Mustang that has been re-vamped.

The outer trappings of a character speak volumes to the personality of the individual.

Writers are always admonished to "show" and not just simply "tell."

What better way to show the reader a lot about the character than by their dress and the possessions they own and value.

Think about James Bond or Columbo. Their wardrobes help define their character.

Heroine - Kayla

Kayla has a very conservative wardrobe mainly consisting of blue jeans and lots of plain tops — only one black dress to her name.

Why is this important?

She would love to wear brighter and bolder colors but her husband told her she looked like a cheap whore in them.

Hero - Quinn

Quinn's wardrobe is very basic. Lots of sweats. Dark blue pants and shirts with pockets — only one suit and a few dress shirts for when he has to appear in court.

Why is this important?

Quinn dresses in suits when he has to. He is casual the rest of the time, but he always needs pockets in his shirts for a small notebook and pen he carries.

Villain - Emily

She loves expensive jewelry, especially if it is made of silver or gold.

Why is this important?

Her jewelry and how witnesses remember it will be an important clue in her capture. Jewelry is a status symbol and a reminder of her valued, prominant place in the medical community.

WARDROBE

Women tend to notice clothing more than men. Depending on whose story it is, the character's wardrobe may or may not be important. In a male oriented action tale, the main character's wardrobe may be mundane or consist of sweats. For women the clothes might be exotic, such as the gowns worn by Padme Admidala in *The Phantom Menace* or Mame in *Auntie Mame*.

In most novels, what the character wears, whether at work, at play, or even sleeping gives the reader an immediate grasp on that character's personality and perhaps occupation. Clothes help the reader's mental image of the character, but accessories such as watches, necklaces, and even a diamond tiara can be important.

How about shoes? Remember V. I. Warshawski's red heels and how she met the doomed hero?

His patterned plastic soles left a distinctive trail in the freshly fallen snow. His flip-flops made squishy noises as he strode across the galley. She made it a point to always match her socks to her Birkenstocks. Is she always in denims and sandals? Does he favor silk shirts and Italian loafers or washed-out jeans and ratty sneakers? Think of the sexual tension you can give a story just with shoes!

Also, how does your character take care of his or her clothes? Is she messy or neat? How about style? Conservative, cheap, second-hand, classic, casual, or practical? What goes with these clothes? A briefcase, backpack, or a fanny pack? Are the clothes color-coordinated or just haphazardly thrown on with no regard for matching hues or textures? Clothes can give the reader or viewer great insight into the makeup of the character.

EXERCISES

- Go through any magazine. Find an interestingly dressed man or woman, either stylishly or casually dressed. Now write a paragraph about this person's personality based on his or her clothes.

- Your character, who has been wealthy all her life, suddenly is penniless. How is she going to emotionally adjust to her new clothing standards when all she can afford are sale items at the Salvation Army thrift store?

- Describe a wardrobe in a movie you just saw that gave you an immediate sense of who that person was. Why did that character have that wardrobe? (Reese Witherspoon in *Legally Blonde*)

Heroine

Character:

Wardrobe:

Hero

Character:

Wardrobe:

Villain

Character:

Wardrobe:

Heroine - Kayla

Kayla tries to tame her unruly hair each morning but usually ends up putting on a hat or scarf to cover her bright, red curls.

Why is this important?

Quinn will encourage her to remove her hat or scarf and show off what he considers her beautiful hair.

Hero - Quinn

Quinn goes to the barber every three weeks to have his hair trimmed. If his hair becomes the least bit long, he feels sloppy and undisciplined.

Why is this important?

It is another indication of his spartan lifestyle.

Villain - Emily

Emily continually washes her hands out of habit and continually slathers lotion onto her hands.

Why is this important?

Because the lotion keeps her hands soft and supple, an important characteristic to show others she's not from a "manual labor" class.

GROOMING

Beyond clothing, a character's grooming habits, or lack thereof, can make him or her stand out in the reader's mind. How about the character who always checks her appearance each time she passes a mirror? Or the character who barely takes time to run a comb or brush through his hair or verifies his clothes match before heading out the door?

- In *Pretty Woman*, Vivian, played by Julia Roberts, was caught flossing her teeth.
- In *Mommie Dearest*, Faye Dunaway played Joan Crawford, a woman obsessed with her personal appearance who meticulously plunged her face into a bowl of water and ice cubes each morning to give a rosy hue to her complexion.
- David Suchet in *Hercule Poirot* has a special mustache wrap he uses while sleeping to preserve his mustache's perfect shape.
- In *As Good As It Gets*, Jack Nicholson as Melvin Udall suffers from a severe obsessive compulsive disorder. After washing his hands, using an individually wrapped bar of soap, he then throws the used bar away.

Personal grooming habits can add a touch of humor or they can help the reader more readily identify themselves with the character. Grooming can include the uses of various aftershaves and perfume, a great hair style or cut, perfect makeup, a clean shave, or even a perfectly trimmed goatee.

Villains, on the other hand, could have dirty unkempt hair and beards; have poor hygiene, and bad breath. Turn their grooming habits around for classy villains.

EXERCISES

- A woman goes to interview for a job in a cosmetic store. She desperately needs the job because she is a single mother with a child to support. However, she has nothing decent to wear and no fashion sense. How will her potential new boss react and how will she convince that person she is the right person for the job?

- A man who has always been meticulous in his grooming habits with an aversion to the outdoors suddenly finds himself stranded on a deserted island far from civilization. How will he react?

- Think about a character in a movie you saw recently who had a quirky grooming habit. Why did this habit endear you to that character?

Heroine

Character:

Grooming:

Hero

Character:

Grooming:

Villain

Character:

Grooming:

Heroine - Kayla

She has no car, but rides a bike everywhere.

Why is this important?

Her husband had limited her freedom by controlling her use of the car. She learned to ride a bike and now rides to get in shape.

Hero - Quinn

Quinn's vehicle is a flatbed truck.

Why is this important?

Because he is a practical man. The truck can be used to haul things like groceries or supplies for the deck he is building on the back of his house — but he longs for a bike, a Harley Davidson.

Villain - Emily

A BMW sports car for driving to the hospital.

Why is this important?

This reveals her need for expensive items. The car is fast and she is caught speeding.

VEHICLE(S)

Beyond clothing, a character's vehicle can tell the reader or viewer something about who that person is. Perhaps she owns a convertible. Does he drive a four-wheel drive sports utility van or a Jaguar?

She rides a ten-speed bike, he has a vintage Harley Davidson hog. He uses his plane every day to check his ranch, while she roller blades to the office. She sails her yacht on the weekend, while he canoes downstream. He rides the bus into work while she takes a taxi.

What part will the vehicle play in the story? Is it needed in the climax to save someone? James Bond was forever in trains, ski lifts, space vehicles, and cars with gadgets. All were important in getting him out of tricky situations.

Let's not forget the Batmobile, the starship *Enterprise*, and all those exotic machines such as the *Red October* submarine or the hot air balloon used in *Around the World in 80 Days*. All these vehicles help with the character's movements and contribute to the action and the story setting.

Then there are the animals used for transportation. Animals such as horses, donkeys, camels, mules, and elephants are fairly normal, but when you write science fiction you are only limited by your imagination.

If you are writing historicals, be sure you are true to the times and research the types of wagons, carriages, buggies, or Model Ts that were used.

The type, size, color, shape, and design of the vehicle all give the reader or viewer important insight into the character's persona and in many cases, especially in action movies where high-speed car chases are the norm, the vehicle needs to be equipped with the latest technological advances.

EXERCISES

- On a world, in an alternative universe, the only mode of transportation is non-motorized. Your character dreams of a better and faster means of travel. What does he or she develop and how does society react to this invention?

- The vehicle has a flat tire. How does a female character react? How does a male character react? (This is a fun place to work on role reversal.)

- Describe and define your character's vehicle. How important will this vehicle be in the story? Only as a means of transportation or as the getaway car?

Heroine

Character:

Vehicle:

Hero

Character:

Vehicle:

Villain

Character:

Vehicle:

Heroine - Kayla

She has always wanted a dog. Now that her husband, who hated animals, is gone, she has decided to adopt a puppy.

Why is this important?

She feels lonely. A puppy represents the beginning of her new life. She adopts an unwanted dog that needs TLC.

Hero - Quinn

Quinn has never had time for a pet because he is never home.

Why is this important?

He doesn't have time to love a pet. Loving a pet means giving emotionally and Quinn doesn't have time or so he tells himself. Besides the pet could die.

Villain - Emily

Emily talks to her cockatoo.

Why is this important?

She vents her frustrations when she talks to the bird. Also, cockatoos are expensive and can be trained to talk. This is a challenge to her intellect.

PET(S)

Whether it is a cat acting as a witch's familiar or a guard dog protecting a mansion, creatures have long played an important part in story telling. Dragons, serpents, or even clown fish have been made into fascinating stories. Hagrid has Fang (dog) and Norbert (baby dragon) in the *Harry Potter* books. Ron has a rat, Harry an owl, and Dumbledore has a phoenix.

Christopher Robin had Winnie the Pooh, while Annie had Sandy. Of course, we all remember Lassie and Rin Tin Tin, but how about the parrot who talks and always seems to have the "answer" that solves the mystery, or the dog who growls at the seemingly nice person, who later turns out to be the villain?

Pets humanize characters. The aggressive business woman may come home to her puppy or kitten and totally spoil it. The lone cowboy talks to his horse, who is his best friend. The alien saves a rabbit from being shot hereby showing the reader he's not all bad.

Having a character explain actions and emotions to a pet in snippets of short dialogue can break up long paragraphs of exposition and reveal some of their inner thoughts and conflicts.

Of course not all pets have to be "real." Writers, through the ages, have made up special creatures for their stories. Fables are full of talking animals and plants. Mythological animals include dragons, trolls, fairies, elves, satyrs, kappa, and Pegasus to mention a few. And cryptozoology (meaning "rumored to actually exist") contains Bigfoot, the Loch Ness monster, Sasquatch, shape shifters, and the Jersey Devil. Let's not forget Harvey, the invisible rabbit from the movie *Harvey* owned by Elwood P. Dowd (Jimmy Stewart), the Cheshire Cat, gremlins, and Rudolph the Red-nosed Reindeer.

EXERCISES

- This character has just lost his beloved dog. How will this affect him emotionally? Will he get another one?

- She roams with the wild beasts calling them by name. Isolated in her part of the world, she communicates with the animals. What happens to her when brought to civilization?

- Did he unwillingly inherit a bad-tempered mongrel (think Tom Hanks in *Turner and Hooch)*. How did he handle the dog?

Heroine

Character:

Pet(s):

Hero

Character:

Pet(s):

Villain

Character:

Pet(s):

MOST PRIZED POSSESSION

A prized possession can say so much about who your character is. A woman who values her grandmother's hope chest is very different from a woman who could care less about heirlooms and wants only the shiniest bauble from Tiffany's. A man who has spent hours restoring a Shelby Mustang is going to be totally different than the man who values the size of his bank account.

A perfect example is the *Gift of the Magi* by O. Henry. Della has long hair that is her most prized possession, while her husband, Jim, treasures the gold watch his father gave him. They each sacrifice their treasure because of their love. She cuts her hair to buy him a chain for his watch, while he pawns his watch to buy her a comb for her hair.

Whether it is a car, the family's dog, or a valuable painting, what your characters value above everything else will say a lot about who they are. A stolen family heirloom might be just what it takes to get an introverted woman to give up her sheltered life and go on a daring adventure.

Think of Arthur's sword "Excaliber," or the Declaration of Independence that Benjamin Gates (Nicolas Cage) is trying to protect in *National Treasure*, or even Billy's dogs in *Where the Red Fern Grows*.

Most prized possessions tend to stay the same, no matter what century you are writing about. Heirlooms of any sort are always valued, as is money, jewelry, paintings, and stamp collections. Legal papers also are greatly prized such as birth and death certificates, passports, and wills. Possessions that have a great personal meaning are also valued such as an autographed baseball, a special musical instrument, a photograph, or even a wedding ring. Think about it. If a fire were to start in your home and you had only minutes to get out, what would you save?

Heroine - Kayla

Kayla's prize possession is a tattered copy of *Pride and Prejudice*.

Why is this important?

Because she admires the character of Elizabeth Bennet and wants to be like her. And the book was given to her by her now deceased aunt.

Hero - Quinn

Quinn's most prized possession is a picture of his mother.

Why is this important?

Even though she died when he was young, the photo reminds him of her gentleness and the way she smelled.

Villain - Emily

A watch she bought for herself when she passed her boards.

Why is this important?

The watch symbolized her intelligence and reminds her she is smarter than most people.

EXERCISES

- This character values his computer and the disks on which he has been working on. His computer crashes or some of his disks are stolen. How will he react?

- The family safe has been broken into. What was taken? How will this character react?

- What is your most prized possession? Why do you value this item? How could you use this item in a story?

Heroine

Character:

Most prized possession:

Hero

Character:

Most prized possession:

Villain

Character:

Most prized possession:

Heroine - Kayla

Kayla is very conservative in the way she dresses and prizes her copy of *Pride and Prejudice*.

Why is this important?

She will experiment with brighter, more stylish clothing and try to be more daring like Elizabeth Bennet in *Pride and Prejudice* in an effort to get Quinn to notice her more as a woman than a suspect.

Hero - Quinn

Quinn's possessions are very simple and what he owns is practical.

Why is this important?

It shows he is used to a simple life and he doesn't bother with frivolous things.

Villain - Emily

All Emily's possessions, including her prized watch, reflect her financial status.

Why is this important?

Because status is the only means Emily uses to measure her self-worth.

SUMMARY

Who a character is can be demonstrated by what they have and what they value. These items don't need to play a big part in the story, but if you know what your characters are wearing and what they like and prize, it will go a long way to thoroughly understanding them. It also gives the reader or viewer a look inside each character's soul without the character having to say a word.

The items can play a role in the story or the final outcome. A person whose smart pet that saves her or him or brings the characters together can make for a fun story. Learning what is a character's most valuable possession and then having them lose or sacrifice that possession can bring a satisfying end as well.

Use this page to list the various aspects of your character's wardrobe and possessions and explain what they mean to the story.

ENVIRONMENT AND DAILY LIVING

STEP EIGHT

OVERVIEW

Now that we have our characters fairly well defined, we need to know how they live and spend their free time. While this information may or may not be used in the overall story, the writer needs to know it. It might be critical if you're telling a "fish-out-of-water" story, where the character is thrown into circumstances and surroundings opposite of her or his normal life.

Home

Your heroine comes home from a long day at work. Does she pour a glass of wine and sit beside the wall of windows in her loft and admire a view of the mountains? Does she throw on a bathing suit and go outside to sit in the hot tub on her deck overlooking the ocean? Or does she go right to her home office and start going through the mail?

Office/Work Place

Does he work in an expensive and excessively neat corner office on the ninety-second floor overlooking the sprawling city or does he work in a small cubicle that is covered with Post-it notes? Perhaps he has a small workroom in the corner of a garage.

Community

How characters interact with their community is also important. Is she just one small worker bee in a large city or a leader in her small rural town?

A Day and a Weekend in the Life of...

It's also time for our characters to "get-a-life." How do they spend their days? Much of this material may be used when building scenes. However, be careful not to use this to simply fill up a sagging middle in your story. Every scene must serve a purpose.

This step is important to help give the reader, and definitely the viewer, a sense of the character's ordinary living conditions which also might include:
- economic status
- era
- life on other worlds

Heroine - Kayla
Kayla lives in an apartment with her husband.
Why is this important?
She has always wanted her own house.

Hero - Quinn
Quinn lives in a small house.
Why is this important?
He bought it because he needed roots, a connection. It's stark; there are no mementos and only a picture of his mother.

Villain - Emily
Emily lives in a high-rise loft.
Why is this important?
She likes to stand in front of the window and look out at the city as she's paid a lot for this view. This is still another status symbol she enjoys.

HOME

A man's home is his castle or so the saying goes, but is it? What if he lives in a one-room shanty or even in a cave in another universe? Perhaps he lives in a small apartment that is cluttered with empty beer cans and discarded pizza boxes. Does he lounge in front of his big screen plasma TV to catch a baseball game? Does he go outside his cabin to chop wood for an evening fire? Home could also be a cardboard box, a train station, or even the back room of a business.

Is your heroine a single young woman who lives in an isolated ranching community in a small log cabin? Perhaps she is a single mother living in the suburbs with her children in a ranch-style home in a new subdivision or maybe in the old family home on a tree-lined street.

Could the villain be a multi-millionaire who lives on a gated estate and keeps a high-rise glass-walled condo in the city? Or does she live in the penthouse of a huge building? Perhaps your character is hiding out in a cave or is an English lord in his castle, or a pioneer in a sod house.

If one is writing in the sci-fi genre or in any of the paranormal genres, home can be anything in the writer's imagination. From underground caves to a city in the clouds, anything goes.

Inside the dwelling, what are the furnishings like? Expensive or cheap? Bought new or hand-me-downs? New and stylish or old-fashioned-looking with dark heavy furniture?

What of the arrangement of the furniture? Is it crowded or sparse? Lots of pieces all over the place so there is no room for games or a loft with only a few strategically placed screens to divide the larger areas?

EXERCISES

- She lives in a one-room loft in the middle of the city. He lives on a huge ranch in the middle of nowhere. They want to marry. Who will move and why?

- He wanders the world, never putting down roots — his home is his backpack. She loves her home in a small community where she knows everyone. They fall in love but where do they settle?

- She still lives with her parents and desperately wants to be on her own. What will her first apartment look like?

Heroine

Character:

Home:

Hero

Character:

Home:

Villain

Character:

Home:

Heroine - Kayla
Kayla takes pride in the apartment she shares with her husband but she doesn't like living there.
Why is this important?
Kayla keeps her place very clean and neat. She has nothing else to fill her time and she also doesn't want to provide her husband with anything else to criticize her for.

Hero - Quinn
Quinn likes the hustle and bustle of the police station.
Why is this important?
It gives him something to focus on rather than the loneliness he feels in his empty house. His desk is an organized mess. However, he can quickly find relevant information for any case he is working on.

Villain - Emily
Emily likes the sterile atmosphere of the O.R.
Why is this important?
Because here, she is in control. Her office is also orderly but sterile. This environment keeps people at arms length.

OFFICE/WORK ENVIRONMENT

Whether it's an operating room or an assembly line, where the character works gives the reader or viewer an opportunity to relate to these surroundings and also to watch the character relate to his or her co-workers and colleagues.

Does the character work for someone else or does he work for himself out of his home, condo, or apartment?

Is your character the boss with the big corner office with all the windows, or is she an underling, trying to get out of her crowded cubicle that she shares with four other people who are constantly interrupting her work?

The work environment played a major role in the movie *Working Girl*, as Tess found herself becoming more and more assertive. In *Office Space*, no one could stand the boss, and the equipment kept breaking down. The audience could relate to the constant demands and the sudden decision to lay people off, which led Peter and his friends to decide to rip off the company. Only the actions of a more disgruntled worker saved them from being caught.

Of course, an office or working space can be anywhere from a small office in a ranch or farm to the back room in a beauty salon or tattoo parlor. Where your main character works will give the reader a better sense of who this character is. Is the space modern, ultra modern, as in a futuristic computer office, or old-fashioned, with a roll-top desk in the back of a small town's general hardware store?

Many workspaces are in the character's home. This can be from the bed-and-breakfast owner to the very private, isolated, and wounded CEO of a huge company.

EXERCISES

- A secretary hears and sees almost everything going on in the office. Late one night she overhears two of her co-workers planning to murder the boss — a man everyone hates. He has been sexually harassing her since she stared working. What does she do?

- A computer hacker taps into his boss's bank account where he discovers that his boss is stealing from the company. What does he decide to do? Does he use his computer skills to put the money back or steal some for himself and make it look like the boss did it?

- A woman decides to try a chat room on her computer and portrays herself as a beautiful, sexy, and outgoing woman. What happens when a man she meets in the chat room wants to meet her in person? How does she react?

Heroine

Character:

Office/Work environment:

Hero

Character:

Office/Work environment:

Villain

Character:

Office/Work environment:

Heroine - Kayla
Kayla lives in an older suburb.
Why is this important?
Insulated from the violence of "downtown," the outside view of her suburb presents a pretty picture while concealing the ugliness of life within the apartment she shares with her husband.

Hero - Quinn
Quinn lives downtown.
Why is this important?
It is close to the precinct and allows him to save dollars for a future rainy day. It also keeps him in tune with current community issues.

Villain - Emily
Emily lives in an elegant loft near the hospital where she works.
Why is this important?
This loft showcases her belief in herself and her belongings, awards, and wealth. It's picture perfect, right out of a magazine.

COMMUNITY

What kind of a community does the character live in? Is it Manhattan's Upper West Side or a ranch in the middle of Montana, fifty miles from any town? Does your character live in a fantasy world, like Batman did in Gotham City? Knowing the answers to these questions can also help flesh out your characters.

How active is your character in the community. Is she interested in clubs or would she prefer everyone simply leave her alone?

Giving your character a location cannot only show who the person is, but the community can play a major role in the story itself. Think of Jim Carrey in *The Truman Show* or Andy Griffith's Mayberry.

How about the big city doctor stuck in a small backwater town, like Michael J. Fox in *"Doc" Hollywood*. Fish out of water stories are popular and wreak havoc for your characters even if the main plot involves a mystery or a romance.

Maybe your character is just dying to get out of a small town. Imagine the trouble he might have in a large city if all he has ever known is country living. How about the English woman that moves to the Wild West?

Communities are not necessarily always towns or cities. A small but interesting group of people can form a bond on a cruise ship, in a gated community, or even on one floor of a college dormitory. Other communities might be a military base, a mobile home park, a commune, or a religious retreat. Large or small, this group of individuals with their unique beliefs and set of rules will impact your character whether she or he is part of the group or fighting to leave.

EXERCISES

- This character lives in the country on a farm. Describe how he deals with a day in the city.

- She is rich and famous and returning home to her small town. How does she react and how do the town's people react to her?

- Describe a movie where community played a big role.

Heroine

Character:

Community:

Hero

Character:

Community:

Villain

Character:

Community:

Heroine - Kayla

She works each day on the classes she is taking online and does household chores. She likes TV movies that reflect a woman struggling toward independence.

Why is this important

Taking online classes means she doesn't have to communicate with anyone directly and encourages her independence.

Hero - Quinn

Quinn gets up to exercise and goes to work at the same time each day and works long hours. He usually comes home late.

Why is this important?

It shows he would rather work than be home alone.

Villain - Emily

Emily has a very ordered life.

Why is this important?

This allows her to stay in control and maintain her privacy.

A DAY IN THE LIFE OF. . .

What about the daily life of your characters? Are they likely to come home straight from work and turn on the TV? Go to a concert or have dinner with friends? Do they stop by the gym every day? Order out, or are they gourmet cooks who love to invite their friends over to share dinner?

The daily life of your characters might not play a large role in the story itself, although it can make a big impact on the character. A small-town minister thrust into the mean streets of Hollywood to look for his daughter is going to see things a lot differently than the street-wise private investigator he might hire to help him.

Knowing how your characters live before the story starts can contribute to the story as well. Throwing your character's world into total disarray is always a fun device, but you need to fully know how your characters live before you can do this.

By filling in the gaps of your character's day-to-day living, you will be able to understand him or her and any underlying problems and motives they may have.

- **Morning**: How does your character wake up? Grumpy or ready to take on the world?
- **Noon**: Does he or she eat lunch out with friends or alone at work and then leaves on time or stays late to finish work?
- **Evening**: Does he or she watch TV or work on a "secret" project; go to bed early, on time, late; watches TV, reads a book; makes phone calls; sleep with someone, etc?

EXERCISES

- Go to dinner with your character. Where will you eat? What kind of a restaurant? A local dive or a hotspot? Who will pick up the check?

- What about breakfast? She loves fresh fruit while he's a potatoes-and-eggs person. Fix them a breakfast that both will like.

- In the movie, *The Wedding Planner*, the heroine spends her days planning weddings and then goes home each evening to eat a TV dinner and watch the *Antiques Road Show* on TV. Why was her evening routine important and how did it endear her to the audience?

Heroine

Character:

A day in the life of:

Hero

Character:

A day in the life of:

Villain

Character:

A day in the life of:

Heroine - Kayla

Kayla spends her weekends trying out new recipes because she likes to cook and dreams of having her own catering service one day. She reads to ill patients at the local hospital.

Why is this important?

She is preparing for her future business. And reading to the sick makes her feel emotionally connected to people who need help.

Hero - Quinn

Quinn does wood carving on the weekends and takes long runs in the country.

Why is this important?

He secretly wants to be an artist. He carves wonderful make-believe animals that he gives to the young cancer patients in a nearby clinic. Running keeps him in shape and provides relaxation.

Villain - Emily

Emily's weekend is pre-planned.

Why is this important?

Once a month she takes a trip out of town to a resort. Her Saturday mornings are for sleeping and massage therapy. This is important because her pattern changes after she murders Kayla's husband.

A WEEKEND IN THE LIFE OF. . .

What does your character do on the weekend? Does he have a secret life or is he a family man who spends the weekend working around the house? Is she a party girl who lives for Friday night or does she dread the weekend because she has nowhere to go and no one to do it with?

Spend a weekend with your character. Would he go to a Mexican beach? Eat exotic food? Would she sit in a cozy bed and breakfast relaxing with a good book? Go water skiing or backpacking? Or perhaps stay home and work on a special project?

Go to a party with your character. Is he the life of the party? Does she hide in the corner? Is he bored? Does she sing with the band because they're playing oldies?

Take your character on a shopping expedition to the place of their choice. Would it be to a mall or to a car lot? A discount store or Saks Fifth Avenue? Bookstore or art gallery? Does she buy anything or just look? Does he hate shopping or love it?

Knowing how your character chooses to spend leisure time is another way to provide depth. Whether she or he spends the weekend alone or with friends and family, it helps define who that character is to your audience.

- **Friday night**: Works, plays, has a date, or stays home?
- **Saturday morning**: Does errands, cleans house, washes clothes?
  Afternoon: Plays a sport, exercises, goes visiting or shopping?
  Evening: Has a date, has no date, throws a dinner party?
- **Sunday morning**: Church, organizes wardrobe, goes for a drive?

EXERCISES

- This character loves parties and even drinks a bit too much on occasion. This weekend she is going to the wedding of her best friend and former boyfriend. What might happen?

- A woman wins a trip to an exotic island in the Caribbean and is caught in a hurricane. How does she react and what happens?

- A man who doesn't spend much time outdoors must take a client who is a camping enthusiast on a backpacking trip to the Australian outback. How does this man react and what could happen?

Heroine

Character:

A weekend in the life of:

Hero

Character:

A weekend in the life of:

Villain

Character:

A weekend in the life of:

Heroine - Kayla

Kayla lives in an apartment in an older suburb with her husband. She keeps it neat and clean so as not to upset her husband. She watches movies about women who are struggling toward independence just like she is.

Why is this important?

After her husband is killed, she will have the freedom to try and spread her wings.

Hero - Quinn

Quinn lives in a house because he wanted roots and a connection that he never had growing up. His garage is full of wood and carving tools.

Why is this important?

The house contains few mementoes and reflects the loneliness he feels. He spends most of his free time in the garage carving his wooden animals.

Villain - Emily

Emily is a creature of predictable habits.

Why is this important?

She is thrown off stride by unexpected complications, which have ramifications in the police investigation.

SUMMARY

While a character's environment does not have to play a major role in a book or movie, it can help the writer understand a character and the character's motivations. Knowing how a character lives and how the character spends his or her time can be used to heighten internal and external conflict.

This isn't a necessary tool, but it can be useful when you're putting your character on paper. When you know what they like and how they live, they can become more real in your head and help you to incorporate those images in your story.

THE CHARACTER DIAMOND

STEP NINE

OVERVIEW

Now that you have your character fairly well developed, it's time to get down to business and decide how this person is going to move through the story. 1) What's going to get him or her started? 2) What will motivate this character to find the answers? 3) What problem will arise and give her or him all sorts of trouble? And finally, 4) How will he or she grow during the course of the story, so that at the end, the character will be a stronger and better person?

There are two elements in each of these four points. For example, if the character's *EXTERNAL complication* is another murdered body, his *INTERNAL complication* might be that the murdered person was also the prime suspect. Or if her *INTERNAL crusade* is to make herself feel more self-confident, then her *EXTERNAL goal* might be to become more assertive.

Since these are four elements that are absolutely necessary to any story, we created the **Character Diamond**.

Remember, all four of these elements must be present for the character to shine as a diamond and be truly memorable.

Crusade

Your character must have a crusade, a goal, a dream. What end result is the character trying to achieve?

Cause

What is causing your character to act? Why does the character want this crusade (or result) so badly?

Complication

What obstacles or stumbling blocks get in the way of the character achieving his or her goal? A problem or complication must arise that your character has to overcome or solve by the end of the story.

Change

How has this character grown or changed by the end of the story? The character must change so that the reader will experience an emotionally satisfying ending to the story.

CRUSADE (WHAT)

At the beginning of a story, there is an inciting incident. Something happens that greatly alters the life of your character. He is falsely convicted of a murder. Her mother suddenly dies. His wife and child are tragically killed. Her small child is kidnapped. All of these are inciting incidents.

This causes the character to go on a CRUSADE to find the answer, to survive, to change jobs, or to go after a dream. The main character in any book, play, movie, or TV show has a goal that he or she will be working toward during the course of the story.

But, no matter what the crusade, goal, or dream is, there are two parts to it. There is the EXTERNAL, which is something that happens in the outside world. This is going to be something physical, such as finding her child's kidnapper, or trying to prove himself innocent of the murder he's accused of committing.

The INTERNAL crusade, or the emotional why, sets the character on his or her path. This is going to come from within the character. It might be trying to prove to herself that she can take care of herself and her child, which is why she personally wants to be involved in solving the kidnapping. Maybe he needs to show that he can outwit the cunning killer using his brain rather than relying on brawn as his only weapon. While the EXTERNAL crusade is tangible, the characters may not even know at the beginning the true reason for the INTERNAL crusade. This may be part of their self discovery through the course of the book.

These goals give the characters something to strive for. Both long- and short-term crusades can be used. Long-term would be the ultimate goal they seek, while short-term goals are the steps that must be accomplished in order for the long-term crusade to be achieved.

Heroine - Kayla

Kayla's EXTERNAL crusade is to prove her innocence.

But her INTERNAL crusade is to become independent.

Hero - Quinn

Quinn's EXTERNAL crusade is to catch the killer.

However, his INTERNAL crusade is to aid justice.

Villain - Emily

Emily's EXTERNAL crusade is not to get caught.

Her INTERNAL crusade is to maintain her respect and flawless surgical record.

EXERCISES

- Think about the last movie you liked. What was the inciting incident that started the character on his or her crusade?

- What were the external and internal crusades of that character?

- Finally, why was this crusade so important to this character?

EXAMPLES

Crusade
(What)

Character	EXTERNAL Crusade	INTERNAL Crusade
Han Solo in the movie *Star Wars*	His goal is to acquire money to pay off his debts to Jabba.	Survival.
Tess McGill in the movie *Working Girl*	She wants to find a better job and make money in the financial world.	To prove to herself and others she can become more than just a secretary and isn't a dumb blonde.
Mr. Fitzwilliam Darcy in the book *Pride and Prejudice*	His goal is to get to know Elizabeth Bennet.	He believes in the superiority of the wealthy and that lack of money is a boundary to people marrying and being in love.
Joan Wilder in the movie *Romancing the Stone*	She must deliver the map.	To save her sister.

Choose a Character from one of your favorite movies:

Character_____

Movie_____

WORKSHEET

Crusade
(What)

This is your page. Fill in the external and internal crusade for each character.

Character	EXTERNAL Crusade	INTERNAL Crusade
Princess Leia in the movie *Star Wars*	Her goal was...	Because...
Jack Trainer in the movie *Working Girl*		
Elizabeth Bennet in the book *Pride and Prejudice*		
Jack Colton in the movie *Romancing the Stone*		

Choose a Character from one of your favorite movies:

Character_____

Movie_____

Heroine

Character:

External crusade:

Internal crusade:

Hero

Character:

External crusade:

Internal crusade:

Villain

Character:

External crusade:

Internal crusade:

Heroine - Kayla

Kayla's EXTERNAL cause is to prove her innocence.

Her INTERNAL cause is that she has been downtrodden too long and doesn't want to go back to her former way of life.

Hero - Quinn

Quinn's EXTERNAL cause is that he doesn't want anyone else to be killed. The killer is dangerous and a threat to society.

His INTERNAL cause is that although he knows Kayla is the prime suspect in the murder, he *believes* she is innocent.

Villain - Emily

Emily's EXTERNAL cause is to cover up her malfeasance.

Her INTERNAL cause is she still feels overlooked by family, friends, and society in general, despite her stellar medical career.

CAUSE (WHY)

If crusade is the "what" of the story, CAUSE is the "why." For each character there has to be both an EXTERNAL and an INTERNAL reason for the character to pursue the goal. Perhaps your heroine's sister is murdered. Her external crusade may be to find the killer. But why? Does she feel guilty because she thinks she might have prevented her sister's death?

The EXTERNAL cause sets her on her course of action. But there must also be an INTERNAL why. What inside her makes her feel guilty? Has she always taken care of her sister and this time she let her down? Is she the oldest child in the family and has had to raise her younger sister because their mother was never around?

Why a character actually pursues a goal is deeper than the crusade setting them off on their current path. The cause is more about the external and internal psyche that underlines the reason(s) a character goes on a crusade. Their course of action may lead them in a certain direction, perhaps into danger, but the reason why they continue forward is their cause.

The CAUSE must be realistic and not over the moon, unless, of course, you are writing sci-fi or paranormal. Also the causes must be relevant to the personality of that individual character. A shy person will do things in a different manner than a stronger, more aggressive individual.

Keep in mind that the internal cause may be like the internal crusade. As long as you, as the writer, know what that character needs to accomplish, you are fine. Perhaps the character realizes it halfway through the story, that they need to overcome a past fear or a past weakness in order to be successful in their cause.

Finally, these causes need to somehow work to help the character realize his/her crusade as they are often closely related.

EXERCISES

- She needs to move on with her life, but somehow can't get past her sister's death. What kinds of internal problems prevent this character from putting the past behind her and moving forward with her life?

- He hates his brother who betrayed him to family and friends, which caused this character to leave home. Tired of wandering, he wants to come home, but lacks the courage. What would motivate or cause him to believe he can finally come to grips with his brother's treachery?

- In the last movie you saw what caused the lead character, both externally and internally to act as he did?

EXAMPLES

Cause
(Why)

Character	EXTERNAL Cause	INTERNAL Cause
Han Solo in the movie *Star Wars*	He wants to pay Jabba so he can stay alive.	He believes that the rebels' cause could get him killed.
Tess McGill in the movie *Working Girl*	She is mistaken for her boss.	She has the chance to prove herself.
Mr. Fitzwilliam Darcy in the book *Pride and Prejudice*	He is drawn to Elizabeth's wit and expressive eyes.	This is the way he was raised.
Joan Wilder in the movie *Romancing the Stone*	Her sister has been kidnapped.	Her sister is the only family she has left.

Choose a Character from one of your favorite movies:

Character_____

Movie_____

WORKSHEET

Cause
(Why)

This is your page. Fill in the external and internal crusade for each character.

Character	EXTERNAL Crusade	INTERNAL Crusade
Princess Leia in the movie *Star Wars*	Her reason was...	Because...
Jack Trainer in the movie *Working Girl*		
Elizabeth Bennet in the book *Pride and Prejudice*		
Jack Colton in the movie *Romancing the Stone*		

Choose a Character from one of your favorite movies:

Character_____

Movie_____

Heroine

Character:

External cause:

Internal cause:

Hero

Character:

External cause:

Internal cause:

Villain

Character:

External cause:

Internal cause:

Heroine - Kayla

Kayla's EXTERNAL complication is being accused of murder and being arrested.

Her INTERNAL complication is guilt over her lack of emotional concern regarding her dead husband and her growing attraction to and feelings for Quinn.

Hero - Quinn

Quinn's EXTERNAL complication is that when someone tries to kill Emily, the evidence points to Kayla.

His INTERNAL complication is that he doesn't trust his emotions because he is falling for Kayla.

Villain - Emily

Emily's EXTERNAL complication is that some of her patients keep dying and the medical authorities are getting suspicious.

Her INTERNAL complication is that she is starting to panic and begins using even more drugs and making more uncharacteristic mistakes.

COMPLICATION (PROBLEM)

The COMPLICATION is the problem that arises for our hero or heroine during the course of their crusade. This can be anything from an emotional issue, such as a difference of values and beliefs, to an outside physical force threatening to keep them from accomplishing their goal such as an earthquake or robbers stealing their equipment.

Problems can be an impending natural disaster they're fighting against or a villain who is working at every turn to make certain they don't reach their goal. While that may be the EXTERNAL complication, there must be something INTERNAL that is also keeping the hero or heroine from getting what they want. This internal problem could be something from their past, a way of thinking, a strong religious belief, set of values, or a secret. This is a good place to use fears and weaknesses.

Remember, the obstacles must create either danger, betrayal, or a serious threat to one of the character's strong beliefs. Usually, the further along a plot is the more intense the complications and those bigger problems tend to have more at stake!

A complication can also be in the action (external) and/or in the relationship (internal). The most memorable stories have them in both, with one feeding off the other.

To summarize, the external complication will be the viable problem that your characters face. The internal problem stems from something inside the character. This is why it is so important to know the inner feelings of your characters, from their core beliefs to their greatest fears and weaknesses. The readers want to feel that your characters are challenged and severely tested. When they are able to prevail at the end, it makes the story much more satisfying.

EXERCISES

- She is a minister. He is a handyman working on remodeling her church and a recovering alcoholic who has lost his faith in everything. When presented with a major crisis, someone keeps trying to bomb the church, how will these two fight the problem?

- He is a cop. She is a cop in Internal Affairs trying to prove he is dirty and tampered with evidence to have someone convicted. When her life is threatened, how do they work together to discover who is responsible?

- In the last movie or book you liked what complication arose that presented a real sticky problem, both internally and externally, for the main character?

EXAMPLES

Complication
(Problem)

Character	EXTERNAL Complication	INTERNAL Complication
Han Solo in the movie *Star Wars*	The bounty hunters want him dead.	He has begun to care about the rebels.
Tess McGill in the movie *Working Girl*	Her boss suddenly appears.	She is not able to stand up for herself.
Mr. Fitzwilliam Darcy in the book *Pride and Prejudice*	He knows that Elizabeth despises him because of his proud, arrogant nature.	He falls in love with Elizabeth, a woman he believes is beneath his social status.
Joan Wilder in the movie *Romancing the Stone*	She doesn't know if she can trust Jack, and people are trying to kill her.	She is unsure if she should trust Jack and she is falling in love with him.

Choose a Character from one of your favorite movies:

Character_____

Movie_____

WORKSHEET

Complication
(Problem)

This is your page. Fill in the external and internal complication for each character.

Character	EXTERNAL Complication	INTERNAL Complication
Princess Leia in the movie *Star Wars*	Her problem was...	Because...
Jack Trainer in the movie *Working Girl*		
Elizabeth Bennet in the book *Pride and Prejudice*		
Jack Colton in the movie *Romancing the Stone*		

Choose a Character from one of your favorite movies:

Character_____

Movie_____

Heroine

Character:

External complication:

Internal complication:

Hero

Character:

External complication:

Internal complication:

Villain

Character:

External complication:

Internal complication:

Heroine - Kayla

Kayla's EXTERNAL change is that she is cleared of all charges.

Her INTERNAL change is that she becomes confident and independent.

Hero - Quinn

Quinn's EXTERNAL change is that he is injured saving Kayla who was confronted by Emily.

His INTERNAL change is that he is now capable of accepting and giving love.

Villain - Emily

Emily's EXTERNAL change is that she is incarcerated.

Her INTERNAL change is that she blames Kayla and Quinn and vows revenge.

CHANGE (END RESULT)

During the journey, a memorable character changes, grows, and matures to become a different person by the end of the story. Perhaps he has learned that trust is a two-way street. Or she has found the inner strength that allowed her to shoot the villain.

Dorothy in the *Wizard of Oz* learned "there's no place like home" and true friends are priceless. Han Solo in *Star Wars* changed from a man wanting only to save his own skin to a true hero who helped others. His selfish desire for reward matured into realizing the higher value of love, friendship, and even the survival of independence.

At some point, usually toward the end of the story, the character has to realize that if she doesn't do something different all will be lost. With this realization comes the permanent CHANGE of their outlook. Villains don't really change much, they either stay the same or get worse.

Again, there are both EXTERNAL and INTERNAL changes in store for your characters. The external will be the realization of their crusade. She solves the case or he saves his children. The internal change will be much more subtle, but it is still there. She realizes she is strong enough to do things on her own, or like Joan Wilder in *Romancing the Stone*, who tells her editor she has become a "hopeful romantic."

One way to illustrate CHANGE is to show the person who hated children now playing with his kids, or having a terribly shy person now giving a lecture. Perhaps the mean person becomes kinder. Remember Scrooge in *A Christmas Carol*? Oftentimes this change is called the "character arc." This refers to the change the character makes from the beginning of the story through to the end.

EXERCISES

- She needs to get a job to keep a roof over her head but she's over fifty with no work history. How does she change?

- He lost his hand in an industrial accident. How does he feel at the beginning of the story? How does he change by the end? (Nicolas Cage in *Moonstruck*)

- Think of a villain who changed for the worse. Where was s/he at the beginning of the story and by the the final moments of the tale?

EXAMPLES

Change
(End Result)

Character	EXTERNAL Change	INTERNAL Change
Han Solo in the movie *Star Wars*	Han returns to help Luke destroy the Death Star.	He finally realizes that people are more important than money.
Tess McGill in the movie *Working Girl*	Tess confronts her boss and explains her ideas to the client.	She finally believes in her own strengths and abilities.
Mr. Fitzwilliam Darcy in the book *Pride and Prejudice*	He marries Elizabeth despite her social standing and her family.	He becomes more sensitive to others and their feelings.
Joan Wilder in the movie *Romancing the Stone*	She faces General Zolo and saves herself and her sister.	She changes from a "hopeless" romantic into a "hopeful" romantic.

Choose a Character from one of your favorite movies:

Character_____

Movie_____

WORKSHEET

Change
(End Result)

This is your page. Fill in the external and internal change for each character.

Character	EXTERNAL Change	INTERNAL Change
Princess Leia in the movie *Star Wars*	Her change was...	Because...
Jack Trainer in the movie *Working Girl*		
Elizabeth Bennet in the book *Pride and Prejudice*		
Jack Colton in the movie *Romancing the Stone*		

Choose a Character from one of your favorite movies:

Character_____

Movie_____

Heroine

Character:

External change:

Internal change:

Hero

Character:

External change:

Internal change:

Villain

Character:

External change:

Internal change:

Heroine - Kayla

- Crusade
  External - prove innocence
  Internal - become
  independent
- Cause
  External - jail is a possibility
  Internal - wants a new life
- Complication
  External - accused of murder
  Internal - falls for Quinn
- Change
  External - is proven innocent
  Internal - becomes confident

Hero - Quinn

- Crusade
  External - to solve the crime
  Internal - to right a wrong
- Cause
  External - stop the killings
  Internal - thinks she
  is innocent
- Complication
  External - thinks she is
  guilty
  Internal - his attraction
  to Kayla
- Change
  External - injured saving
  Kayla
  Internal - is capable of love

Villain - Emily

- Crusade
  External - avoid capture
  Internal - maintain
  respect/trust
- Cause
  External - murdered Kayla's
  husband
  Internal - feels overlooked
- Complication
  External - authorities
  suspicious
  Internal - panic, more
  drug use
- Change
  External - incarceration
  Internal - vows revenge

SUMMARY

Heroine
CRUSADE
- External
- Internal

CAUSE
- External
- Internal

COMPLICATION
- External
- Internal

CHANGE
- External
- Internal

Hero
CRUSADE
- External
- Internal

CAUSE
- External
- Internal

COMPLICATION
- External
- Internal

CHANGE
- External
- Internal

Villain
CRUSADE
- External
- Internal

CAUSE
- External
- Internal

COMPLICATION
- External
- Internal

CHANGE
- External
- Internal

PUTTING IT ALL TOGETHER

OVERVIEW

We've come to the end of the book. And it's time to put all the information we have gathered about each of our three characters into one or two pages and really make them come alive. On the following pages we have done just that. Going back through the book and laying the sidebars side by side, we have created some interesting facts about these three people.

Kayla   Our sympathies are with her as she has suffered the most, yet, she has also grown the most.

Quinn   He also has changed — going from being a "loner" to being in love and deeply caring for another person.

Emily   Unfortunately, she has only gotten worse.

At last, the characters are almost finished. Notice we say almost. The final touches will occur as the story progresses.

There will be changes. They might be physical changes that are needed for the plot, or more than likely, different skills or talents will be added to the character as needed to reflect plot changes.

All of these factors will not be known until you are actually writing the story. In some cases there will be emotional changes that will happen to your characters as you get to know them.

One more note. To help keep track of all the various names, both first and last names, we strongly suggest you use some type of an Alphabet Chart, such as the one we have done for our characters. Recording the names, whether they be the deceased characters used only off-screen, or important secondary characters keeps you on track and helps avoid character confusion.

When we applied the Alphabet Chart to our story, we had four names all starting with S! See the sidebar. This chart helps the writer keep all the various names from sounding and looking alike.

Alphabet Chart

A - Agnes - Quinn's mother
B - Byron - Kayla's husband
C - Chester, M.D.
    - Wade's last name
D
E - EMILY
F - Frank - Quinn's father
G
H - Hector - Quinn's partner
I
J - Johnson - Professor to Emily
K - KAYLA
L
M - Minton - Emily's last name
N
O
P
Q - QUINN
R
S - Salazar - Quinn's last name
T - Turner - Kayla's last name
U
V
W - Wade - Medical Director
X
Y
Z - Zack - Kayla's dog

Heroine - Kayla

Highlights:

Physical Description
- Curvy with flaming red hair

Profession or Occupation
- Homemaker

History
- Middle-class family
- Oppressed by her parents
- Won a scholarship

Relationships
- Mother deceased
- Estranged from father and his new wife
- No best friend

Personality
- Quiet and goes along with other people's suggestions

Body Language and Speech
- Fidgets when faced with controversy
- Chatty when she's upset

Wardrobe and Possessions
- Conservative clothes, no car
- Adopts puppy

Environment and Daily Living
- Lives quietly except for her trips to the library or reading to patients at the hospital

Character Diamond
- CRUSADE
  - prove innocence
  - nurture independence
- CAUSE
  - doesn't want to go to jail
  - doesn't want to go back to her former way of life
- COMPLICATION
  - accused of murder
  - feels guilty over lack of emotion concerning her husband's death and her attraction to Quinn
- CHANGE
  - she is cleared of charges
  - becomes more confident and independent.

KAYLA

Putting It All Together

Kayla is a shy woman who has no self-confidence. While sad that her husband is dead, she is emotionally glad to be rid of him although a bit guilty about her feelings.

She becomes hesitant to form any new relationship. Her reactions to his death make her appear cold and uncaring and cast suspicion on her in regards to his death. When she meets Quinn he is the first man she really trusts, is open with, and feels connected to in a positive manner.

Kayla is attracted to Quinn but wants to nurture her budding independence because she was oppressed by her husband (and her father) for so long. She also sees herself as unattractive, plump, and unloved. Her greatest fear is that now that her husband is dead she will be forced to move back in with her father and stepmother. However, she doesn't want to go back to her former way of life.

Her husband's murder jerks her out of her comfort zone. When she is accused of his murder she needs to be assertive in her own defense. So when faced with the prospect of going to jail she begins to ask the hospital staff questions about her husband and discovers things about him she didn't know.

Kayla discovers that her husband lied consistently about the hospital staff and the care of patients. He was found snooping in personnel files and cash from staff members wallets turned up missing. She was told by a staff member that they saw him talking with Emily on several occasions and they seemed to be arguing about something.

When the police search Kayla's house and discover the second diamond butterfly earring, the mate of the earring found next to her dead husband, the prospect of jail looms even darker. But when Quinn tells her he doesn't believe she killed her husband, for the first time in her life she feels that someone is truly on her side. This new feeling helps build her self-confidence and her growing independence that she can make it on her own.

Kayla points out to Quinn that Emily is always seen wearing expensive jewelry and that perhaps the earring may belong to her. Kayla helps Quinn research Emily's most recent jewelry purchases and together they discover the earring belongs to Emily.

When Kayla is cleared of all charges even though she has grown to love and respect Quinn, she is determined to enjoy her newly found self-confidence and independence.

REVIEW OF KAYLA

Step One — **Physical Description**
Kayla is twenty-eight, slightly above average height, and curvy in all the right places. She has curly red hair, green eyes, with a peaches-and-cream complexion and never wears makeup.

Step Two — **Profession or Occupation**
Kayla doesn't have much of a work ethic because she has never held a paying job.

Step Three — **History**
Kayla was the only child in a structured middle-class family where all the decisions were made by her father. Kayla won a small scholarship that she never got to use. When a stray dog moved into her house and her husband forced her to get rid of it, that was the last straw that made her realize she couldn't go on with her marriage.

Step Four — **Relationships**
Kayla's mother was killed when she was young and when her father re-married a woman with other children, Kayla felt left out and abandoned. Basically a shy person, she never really had a best friend until she met Quinn who was the first person she could really talk to.

Step Five — **Personality**
She generally goes along with other people's opinions and suggestions and isn't used to standing up for herself. She bites her nails when she is nervous. But her strength is that she can adapt to almost any situation which has helped her endure her marriage. Her greatest fear is that now that her husband is dead she will be forced to move back in with her father and stepmother. Unfortunately, she sees herself as plump and unloved.

Step Six — **Body Language and Speech**
Kayla not only fidgets when faced with controversy, but tends to rattle on and often uses the phrase *"You don't know the half of it."*

Step Seven — **Wardrobe and Possessions**
A closet full of blue jeans and lots of plain tops, with only one black dress to her name. She has no car and rides her bike everywhere. Now, alone, she has adopted a puppy.

Step Eight — **Environment and Daily Living**
Kayla lives in an apartment but has always wanted a house. She is a very neat person and keeps her place extremely clean and well organized.

Step Nine — **Character Diamond**
Kayla wants to nurture her budding independence because she has been oppressed for so long. She doesn't want to go back to her former way of life. When she is accused of murdering her husband, she feels guilty over her lack of emotion and concern not only regarding his death but also over her growing attraction to Quinn. She is finally cleared of all charges and even though she has grown to love Quinn, she is determined to enjoy her newly found confidence and independence.

Hero - Quinn

Highlights:

Physical Description
- Tall, physically fit

Profession or Occupation
- Homicide detective

History
- Had an abusive father
- Joined the Army at 18,
- Attended the police academy

Relationships
- Mother deceased
- Has a partner/friend
- No love interest

Personality
- Quiet
- Analytical

Body Language and Speech
- Speaks quietly and to the point

Wardrobe and Possessions
- Basic clothing
- Picture of mother

Environment and Daily Living
- Small house in the middle of an older downtown area

Character Diamond
- CRUSADE
  - to catch the killer
  - to help the underdog

- CAUSE
  - prevent more killings
  - believes Kayla is innocent

- COMPLICATION
  - new evidence points to Kayla's guilt
  - his attraction to Kayla

- CHANGE
  - injured saving Kayla
  - capable of accepting and giving love

QUINN

Putting It All Together

Quinn Salazar has always lived his life as a loner. He leads a simple life and sees things as black and white. He wants to help people, and put the bad guys in jail, but he would prefer to keep everyone at arm's length.

He's never really had anyone get close to him, and he'd just as soon keep it that way. He doesn't want complications in his neat and orderly life. The only mess he wants in his life is crime, because he knows how to deal with that.

When Kayla comes into his life and he begins to find himself caring for her, he is worried. He doesn't want to care about her, but he senses that she is innocent and wants to help her. He tells himself he is doing it to see that justice is done, but he can't help but be attracted to her, too.

Quinn has always believed in helping the underdog and that is how he sees Kayla. No one believes her and he finds all the evidence against her a little too perfect. He doesn't believe in coincidence, and she seems like an easy target.

Once he decides she is innocent, he is bound and determined to help her, despite warnings from his partner that he might put his job and his future in jeopardy. He likes the idea of helping the helpless, but begins to worry about his personal feelings for her.

On that matter, Hector (his partner) has different thoughts. He is pleased to see Quinn finally expose a more human side and he likes the idea that Kayla is bringing out that side of him. Hector hopes she can make Quinn more human; he also hopes she doesn't destroy his friend in the process.

Quinn begins to discover that Kayla is important to him and eventually must make choices that will either let her into his heart or separate her from him for good.

During the course of the action he realizes he doesn't want to lose her and he also discovers that he has a kind heart and will not end up like his drunken abusive father.

He learns Kayla has the ability to draw out the best in him and he is able to open his heart to love for the first time and to continue in life as a more complete person.

REVIEW OF QUINN

Step One — **Physical Description**

Quinn is physically fit, athletic. His hair is military style, his face clean shaven. He has a broken nose and a small scar on the side of his face.

Step Two — **Profession or Occupation**

He is a police officer who works hard at his job as a homicide detective. He has an excellent work ethic and is always ready to tackle the tough jobs or take an extra shift. He's the go-to guy for Homicide. His co-workers and superiors know they can count on him to do a good job and respect him.

Step Three — **History**

Raised by an abusive father, Quinn has worried he will become like him and has avoided any sort of personal relationships. He never knew his mother, who died when he was four, or his grandparents. He's never had anyone close to share his problems or to celebrate his successes.

Step Four — **Relationships**

Quinn is a loner who has never felt the need for company. He spends his off time by himself and seldom socializes with anyone except his partner, and then only under duress. He would rather be cut off from the world than to risk being hurt or losing his temper and becoming abusive like his father.

Step Five — **Personality**

Quinn is independent and his own person. He isn't influenced by others and sees the world in terms of black and white or right and wrong. There are no shades of gray in his thinking. He leads a disciplined life and has problems dealing with people who complain about things but don't try to fix them. As an analytical thinker, he is quick on his feet and because of his background as an abuse victim he believes in helping the underdog. He is a take-charge sort of person who can be very stubborn. He never gets emotionally involved, but he finds himself helping Kayla when he decides she might be innocent. Even though everyone else is convinced of her guilt, he is stubborn enough to stick up for her. At the same time he fears he might get her hurt.

Step Six — **Body Language and Speech**

Sparse. He speaks quietly, but forcefully, and always gets right to the heart of the matter. A man of few words.

Step Seven — **Wardrobe and Possessions**

He wears casual clothing, and owns one nice suit for court. He owns few possessions.

Step Eight — **Environment and Daily Living**

He has a small house which has a workout room in the basement and a wood shop in the garage.

Step Nine — **Character Diamond**

His crusade is to find the killer. He believes in justice so he wants to see that the killer is caught. His cause is that he doesn't want anyone else killed, but at the same time he begins to think that Kayla is innocent and his cause becomes a need to help her prove her innocence. He runs into complications with his work in helping her and within himself because he knows he should not become involved with her on anything more than an impersonal level. Finally, he does solve the crime, but he discovers that not everything is black and white and he learns that he is not cold-hearted like his father. He is capable of accepting and giving love.

Villain - Emily

Highlights:

Physical Description
- A plain Jane with brown hair done in stylish cut

Profession or Occupation
- Trauma surgeon, head of E.R.

History
- Middle child, ignored by parents, encouraged by teachers

Relationships
- Best friend tragically killed, no significant other

Personality
- Persistent, sensitive, worries, drug addicted, private, arrogant, intelligent

Body Language and Speech
- Graceful, poised, calm
- *"Don't worry. You're in good hands."*

Wardrobe and Possessions
- Expensive clothes, jewelry, car, and pet

Environment and Daily Living
- Keeps to herself, likes a sterile, noncomplicated environment with little interpersonal contact

Character Diamond
- CRUSADE
  - avoiding capture
  - maintain respect and trust

- CAUSE
  - cover up guilt
  - fear of getting caught

- COMPLICATION
  - authorities suspicious
  - greater drug addiction and panic

- CHANGE
  - incarceration
  - vows revenge against Kayla and Quinn

EMILY

Putting It All Together

Although Emily is from a mid-sized family, she has spent most of her young life feeling alone. Early on, she learned the power of her mind was what was going to get her places. Winning a scholarship confirmed her belief in her intelligence. The loss of her good friend, through what she considers the ineptitude of the local hospital, influenced her to become a trauma doctor.

For many years, Emily has striven to be the best emergency room doctor in town. Her perfectionism is legendary.

Emily is an intelligent woman with a lot of emotional baggage. Pretty in her own right, she's always believed she was mediocre in looks. Her lack of a significant other has only confirmed this in her mind.

The pressure of her job caused Emily to turn to drugs. Unfortunately, her addiction is affecting her work. When one of her patients goes into an irreversible coma, she panics and kills the man, fearing her drug use will be discovered. Hoping to calm her nerves and regain control of her emotions, Emily breaks into the surgical pharmacy, only to be caught by Kayla's husband.

When he tries to blackmail her, she concocts his demise. Her southern background aids in the effort to remain calm and serene although she's afraid of being caught. When the police don't initially suspect her, she relaxes her guard and believes she is superior to the detective assigned to the case.

A large butterfly diamond earring is lost, later found in the pocket of Kayla's deceased husband.

When Emily discovers the police have the match to her earring, she gets in her BMW and speeds toward a remote area to dispose of her half of the pair. She is pulled over for speeding, going in excess of eighty miles per hour on a rainy road.

Deciding to frame Kayla, she plants the earring in Kayla's house, increasing the odds of the police believing Kayla is the murderer. Her insistence on her privacy leads Quinn to question her and her activities more closely. Quinn discovers Emily purchased the earrings at an expensive jewelry shop.

Caught, Emily can't believe people of inferior intelligence and upbringing have managed to trap her. She vows revenge on the former suspect and her policeman lover, jealous they have achieved an undeserved, close relationship despite the overwhelming circumstantial evidence against Kayla.

REVIEW OF EMILY

Step One — **Physical Description**

Forty-three, petite, short brown hair, and amber eyes, with a few faint acne scars on her face which has made her self-conscious.

Step Two — **Profession or Occupation**

Emergency room doctor who carefully limits her patient load.

Step Three — **History**

Middle child from an upper-class family, she was encouraged to pursue a medical career by a caring teacher. As a top trauma surgeon it gives her access to drugs and methods of murder.

Step Four — **Relationships**

She has always struggled for attention and acceptance. A person her parents viewed as an outsider is the only one who accepts her for who she is, and that friend is tragically killed. Alone and isolated, Emily blames others for her lack of connection. She resents those who have the love and support of friends and family because she feels she deserves love and support more than they do.

Step Five — **Personality**

Emily is obsessed with privacy and won't leave anyone alone in her office. Afraid of being caught with drugs in her office, she works to keep colleagues and the police at a polite distance. She believes she is far superior to them intellectually. Her carefully poised exterior and over-confidence make Quinn re-examine Emily as a suspect.

Step Six — **Body Language and Speech**

Her body language, speech (*"You're in good hands"*), and identifying tags all hide the violent, drug-addicted killer she's become. This keeps suspicion away from her for a long time.

Step Seven — **Wardrobe and Possessions**

Emily purchases expensive items to show off her self-worth to the community. These distinctive items will help identify her later. Even her bird will unwittingly aid in her capture.

Step Eight — **Environment and Daily Living**

She keeps to herself, but makes sure she's mentioned in the high-society gossip columns.

Step Nine — **Character Diamond**

Emily wants recognition from her family and recognition for her talent from the medical community because she's never felt loved by her family. She strives to be the most important doctor at the hospital and perhaps in the city, but people die. Kayla's husband saw her commit the crime of stealing drugs.

Quinn investigates Emily and this causes her to become nervous and even more dependent on drugs. Finally, she is caught and jailed, where she becomes infamous rather than famous. Not only does she blame Quinn and Kayla for her incarceration, she vows revenge.

Heroine - Kayla

When Kayla is accused of murder she wants to prove her innocence to avoid going to jail. She wants to nurture her budding independence. But her guilt over her lack of emotion in regard to her husband's death and her growing attraction to Quinn complicate her life further. In the end she is cleared of all charges and becomes a more confident and independent woman.

Hero - Quinn

Although Kayla is the prime suspect, Quinn believes she is innocent and he shouldn't get involved with her. The case and his personal feelings are complicated further when he finds new evidence linking Kayla directly to the murder. He doesn't trust his emotions because he is falling in love with Kayla. When Quinn is injured saving Kayla's life he realizes that he is capable of accepting and giving love.

Villain - Emily

While she tries to maintain the respect and trust she has from her patients, Emily hides her guilt. She needs to feel important because she feels overlooked by her family and society. As her patients keep dying, Quinn becomes suspicious. Emily's life is further complicated when she panics and begins using more drugs. Her killing spree ends when she is incarcerated. As a result, she vows revenge.

SUMMARY

Now you need to pull together all your notes about your character and give a short synopsis of how the character moves through the story.

Character:
- Physical Description
- Profession or Occupation
- History
- Relationships
- Personality
- Body Language and Speech
- Wardrobe and Possessions
- Environment and Daily Living
- Character Diamond
  CRUSADE
  - external
  - internal

  CAUSE
  - external
  - internal

  COMPLICATION
  - external
  - internal

  CHANGE
  - external
  - internal

- Putting It All Together

FINAL THOUGHTS

OVERVIEW

We are nearing the end of our look at how to develop memorable characters, but there are still a few odds and ends we need to discuss. These are geared toward helping you fully round out your book or movie.

Secondary Characters

Of course, unless you are writing about a hermit, there will be other characters in your story: lovers, friends, enemies, and those characters that are needed to simply move the story or action along, or perhaps needed to help explain your main character's background and motives for doing what she or he is doing in the story. These are the main character's close friends, lover, and perhaps his or her partner.

Off-Screen Characters

In order to help explain your character's motives, you need to delve into their background. This is where you might need to bring to the reader's attention what effect his mother's death had on him when she died giving birth. Perhaps your hero's wife and small child were killed in a tragic car accident and he doesn't want to get married again.

Different Genres

How your characters will act and what their motivations might be will to a certain extent, depend on the genre you are writing. A paranormal story has much more leeway than say, a historical tale where the writer has to stay with what was current in those times.

Personal Thoughts

Finally a few thoughts on writing in general.

Although each of us approaches the development of our characters in a slightly different way, all of us go through all the steps listed in this book.

Some might start with the character's personality, while others might want a broader view and are going to begin with creating that character's Diamond.

There is no "right" way and no "wrong" way. Each writer simply has to find "their" way.

Secondary characters

- friend/buddy
- mentor
- enemy or villain
- comic relief
- sub-plot characters
- partner/business associate
- parents
- siblings
- guardian
- cousins, aunts, and uncles
- pets/animals
- child

Great secondary characters:

- Alfred - *Batman and Robin*
- Friar Tuck - *Robin Hood*
- Nemo's father - *Finding Nemo*
- The donkey - *Shrek*
- Q - *James Bond* series
- Chewbacca - *Star Wars*
- Mary Jane - *Spiderman*
- Hermione - *Harry Potter*
- Fraiser - *Cheers*
- Kramer - *Seinfeld*
- Jake - *Two and a Half Men*

In our story, our secondary characters play an important role with each of the main characters.

Hector — is Quinn's partner and plays the role of a confidant.

Wade — the Medical Director of the hospital begins to suspect Emily and turns the spotlight of the investigation on her.

Zack — Kayla's adopted puppy. His role is also that of a confidant.

SECONDARY CHARACTERS

Secondary characters can make or break a novel. Like condiments on your food, they add flavor and spice to your story. But they must serve a purpose. Secondary characters should either complicate the story or shed light on the main character.

Think of some of the great secondary characters and their importance becomes obvious. What would *Casablanca* be without Sam and his piano? He knew Rick's passion for Ilsa and the importance of Paris.

Colonel Nathan Jessep is only onscreen for several scenes in *A Few Good Men*, but his part in the storyline changes everything. He ordered a Code Red, but saw nothing wrong with the command because of his extreme sense of honor and duty.

People like Mammy in *Gone With the Wind* can be the person who knows the main character inside and out and can react to their foibles. Alfred is always there for Batman, filling in as the orphaned Bruce Wayne's mentor.

Some secondary characters can get the lead character into trouble, like Frodo's hobbit friends. Still, could he have completed his journey without the assistance of his buddy, Sam?

Keep the secondary characters secondary and do not let them take over the story. Consider the tale of Ashley and Melanie in *Gone With the Wind*. While important to the story, they never became the central characters and stayed mainly in the shadows.

If the secondary character becomes too strong and begins to overshadow the main character, think about giving that character his or her own story in a sequel.

EXERCISES

- The main character has a younger brother who turns out to be very helpful to his older brother in solving the mystery. Decide how he will help and exactly how helpful he should be.

- She has a best friend to whom she tells everything. How will this best friend be used to further the plot? Will she hinder or help the heroine and will that be positive or negative?

- She talks to her cat all the time. What does she tell the cat and how will the role of the cat be important in the story?

Secondary Female

Name:

Role in story:

Secondary Male

Name:

Role in story:

Secondary Villain

Name:

Role in story:

OFF-SCREEN AND WALK-ON CHARACTERS

Off-screen characters are those individuals necessary to the plot, but who may never be seen in the story. They are important and each one will probably have a name and a short history and personality developed.

It might be the mother or father of the main character, who is now dead, but played an important part in developing the character's personality. How about the divorced mate who has turned the main character into a bitter and revenge-driven villain? Think of the title character in *Rebecca*.

Other off-screen characters include:

- the dead body
- the departed grandparents
- the talked-about ghost
- the absent brother
- the estranged mother

Walk-on characters are those people who are never named but are needed for a variety of reasons and are usually referred to by their profession such as the cab driver, the nurse, the waitress, etc.

Other walk-on or minor characters might include:

- the cop
- the maid
- wife/husband
- the driver
- the waitress
- witness
- judge

- salesman
- actress
- life guard
- paramedic
- bartender
- counselor
- teacher

- grandmother
- dancer
- fairy godmother
- the butler
- kids at school
- additional but expendable henchmen

In our story, the off-screen characters include:

Miss Johnson — Emily's professor who became her mentor.

Agnes Salazar — Quinn's mother who, because of her early death, caused Quinn's fear of losing someone if he loved them.

Frank Salazar — Quinn's father who beat him as a child.

And probably Kayla's father, Emily's parents and sister, etc.

EXERCISES

- The cop who finds the body is needed because...?

- Her sister is dead, yet because of the way she died, this character's life is totally changed. Describe the dead sister and how she died.

- The waitress is the killer. How can she be brought into the story without the viewer or reader guessing she is the villain?

Off-screen Female

Name:

Role in story:

Off-screen Male

Name:

Role in story:

Walk-on Character(s)

Names:

Role in story:

When you put your character in a sci-fi, fantasy or paranormal story, be sure to consider:

(the following character elements are taken from Han Solo in *Star Wars*)

Physical Description
- Brown hair, brown eyes, handsome with a crooked smile

Profession or Occupation
- Corellian smuggler and pilot of *Millenium Falcon*

History
- Long career as a smuggler on the fringes of the galaxy. During this time, he has made strong allies and some powerful enemies, including Jabba, the Hut.

Relationships
- He never allows himself to become emotionally involved with women or anyone he does business with.

Personality
- Cocky and self-centered

Body Language and Speech
- He uses a lot of smart remarks and is cynical. He smirks and holds up his hand with a finger pointed when he is angry and trying to make a point or to interrupt someone.

Wardrobe and Possessions
- His clothes are casual and a bit rough.

Environment and Daily Living
- The galaxy

Character Diamond
- CRUSADE
  - needs money

- CAUSE
  - to pay Jabba

- COMPLICATION
  - bounty hunters want him dead

- CHANGE
  - returns to help Luke

CHARACTERS IN DIFFERENT GENRES

Science Fiction, Fantasy, and Stories with Paranormal Elements

Stories involving other worlds or alternate realities need just a touch more work in regards to character. How different would *Lord of the Rings* have been without Gollum, or a reluctant king, or a grumpy dwarf, or a sharp-eyed elf? (*The Return of the King*)

Whether your characters exist in a rich fantasy kingdom complete with dragons or a parallel universe, you as a writer have to take care in creating your characters. Does your vampire have issues with the light or have a conscience about turning others to his lifestyle? These sorts of questions influence the character you develop.

Give them the sort of strengths, education, even clothing that will make their actions and abilities make sense in the realm you've created. Will his wardrobe hinder his acceptance as a rescuer? (*Star Wars*) Can she exist underwater without scuba equipment? (*Watchtowers: Water*) How can Deckard know if the android he is about to retire isn't really a human? (*Blade Runner*)

Considering these types of items as you build your characters will save you countless headaches later on. Attention to this sort of detail will provide solutions to plot issues that creep up. Remember Deckard's Voight-Comp analyzer?

Some character building is universal despite the setting. All characters have a family background of some sort, even if it's sharing their toddler nursery with other infants being shocked into making the choices desired by their caretakers. (*Brave New World*)

Characters have: people who influence them in positive and/or negative ways (Alfred in *Batman Begins*); harbor secret dreams (independence for Rose in *Titanic*); have soft spots (like Ripley for the cat in *Aliens*); and exhibit emotions that are universal no matter what time frame your story is set in. The Death Star and Luke Skywalker's life experience are 100 percent space fantasy, yet who can't relate to the teen ready to take on the world and Luke's sentiments of "Blasting off this rock?"

Consider the universal appeal of your character's emotions to the story and give him or her the appropriate tools — via life history, physical abilities, personality, wardrobe, speech, and relationships with others — to fit the setting and resolve the crisis of the story. Your take will have pertinent details that make sense, while connecting with a contemporary audience.

Remember these characters?

Science Fiction
- Data in *Star Trek the Next Generation*
- Grant in *Fantastic Voyage*

Fantasy
- The Beast in *Beauty and the Beast*
- Storm in *X-Men*

Paranormal
- Kim Novak as a witch in *Bell, Book and Candle*
- Cary Grant as an angel in *The Bishop's Wife*
- Rex Harrison as a ghost in *The Ghost and Mrs. Muir*

Science Fiction

Change your character to fit this genre:

Fantasy

Change your character to fit this genre:

Paranormal

Change your character to fit this genre:

When you put your character in a modern romance or gothic story be sure to consider:

(the following character elements are taken from Cher Gorman's gothic suspense *Wolf Island*, in regard to her heroine, Abigail Chapel)

Physical Description
- Violet eyes, brown hair with reddish-gold highlights and slim build.

Profession or Occupation
- Teacher at an all-girls school in England.

History
- Because of her mother's alcoholism, Abby took care of her sister, Miranda, while they were growing up. Now she can trust her sister's rescue to no one else. She has had a few relationships with men in the past, but none that have lasted.

Personality
- She has a sense of humor, she is reliable and supportive, with a sunny disposition.

Body Language and Speech
- She is British and speaks with a "high" English accent. When she is nervous, she rubs a button on her coat or blouse between her fingers.

Wardrobe and Possessions
- She is a conservative dresser. She lives in a modest cottage in the lake country of England.

Environment and Daily Living
- Castle on Wolf Island off the coast of Maine.

Character Diamond
- CRUSADE
  - Find her sister

- CAUSE
  - Sister has disappeared while hunting ghosts on Wolf Island

- COMPLICATION
  - Devlin and the village people

- CHANGE
  - She learns that no matter what life throws at her, she has the strength to fight her way out.

Modern Romantic Gothic Stories

The Castle of Otranto (1764) by Horace Walpole, later the Earl of Orford, is considered to be the first gothic novel ever written. Although it was vilified by the press, the influence of this work has resonated through the centuries.

Remember *Dragonwyck* by Anya Seton? This book was a national best-seller made into a movie starring Gene Tierney and Vincent Price. Who better to play the naive eighteen year-old Miranda Wells and the intriguing and mysterious Nicholas Van Ryn than these two actors? This story, a classic gothic romance, is about a young woman who is drawn into the fascinating world of the old mansion, Dragonwyck, and its seductive master with his dark and terrible secrets.

Originally, gothic novels had a historical setting particularly the Victorian era. However, over the last few years, with the new surge of interest in the gothic novel, these stories are being given a modern setting.

How does this modern setting affect the basic elements of the gothic novel?

The changes can be seen mostly in regard to the protagonists, in the case of a gothic romance, the hero and heroine. First, the heroine may be a woman in jeopardy but she no longer faints, sobs, or becomes breathless with anxiety and panics at the drop of a hat. She isn't oppressed and lonely. She doesn't willingly put herself in danger by leaving the safety of her room to investigate the sudden fearful noise she hears out in the hall either — especially if she knows a murderer is on the loose.

The heroine of today's gothic is a take-charge modern woman with a strong sense of self but with an underlying vulnerability. She uses her intelligence, her wit, and her strength to overcome the obstacles she finds strewn in her path.

What about the hero? He is no longer the brooding tyrant who demands the heroine marry him, a man she doesn't love or want to spend the rest of her life with, living in his dark, gloomy castle. He is, however, enigmatic, secretive, and reflective. It is these very qualities that draw the heroine to him to try and reveal the tender recesses of his heart. She finds him irresistible and alluring despite her fear that he may be involved in something sinister.

As for the romance element, the modern gothic romance novel needs sizzling sexual tension throughout which ends in a heart stirring powerful love between the hero and heroine.

Remember these characters?
- Ingrid Bergman in *Gaslight*
- Merle Oberon in *Wuthering Heights*
- Joan Fontaine *in Rebecca*
- Catherine Morland in *Northanger Abbey*
- Abigail Chapel in *Wolf Island*
- *Phantom of the Opera*
- *Dracula* by Bram Stoker
- *Frankenstein* by Mary Shelley
- *Jane Eyre* by Charlotte Bronte

Romantic gothic

Change your heroine to fit this genre:

Romantic gothic

Change your hero to fit this genre:

Romantic gothic

Change your villain to fit this genre:

When you put your character in a mystery story be sure to consider:

(the following character elements are taken from Kinsey Millhone in *The Alphabet* series)

Physical Description
- Thin, athletic build, medium height, brown hair that she usually cuts herself

Profession or Occupation
- Private Investigator

History
- Born in Santa Teresa, CA. Her parents were killed in a car accident; raised by her aunt and was rebellious as a teenager.

Relationships
- Few, and prefers to keep it that way. Married twice and divorced. Closest friends are her 80+ landlord and his family.

Personality
- Loner. She is curious and smart, but sometimes her curiosity can get her into trouble.

Body Language and Speech
- Sassy and sharp

Wardrobe and Possessions
- Turtlenecks and jeans; she doesn't care about dressing up. Owns one little black dress. Her car is a VW bug.

Environment and Daily Living
- Lives in a small apartment in a beach community.

Character Diamond
(from *M Is for Malice*)
- CRUSADE
  - She wants to solve a missing-person case

- CAUSE
  - Because she's been hired for the job and needs the money

- COMPLICATION
  - But is confronted with a murder

- CHANGE
  - She starts to let go some of her solitary past

Mystery Stories

Writing characters for mystery novels can be entirely different than writing stand-alone mainstream novels or romances. Often mystery novels evolve into a series and that opens up a whole new realm of character building.

Writing the mystery series can be fun for a writer because the author gets to know their characters very well. The joy is the writer can bring the characters along more slowly and let them go through years of growing and changing.

Yet as a writer, you can't change the main character drastically or immediately or the reader will feel cheated. They've come to know how that character will react in certain situations and they don't expect sudden changes.

Miss Marple is always going to be different than a hard-boiled detective and you wouldn't expect her to suddenly turn up in a singles bar wearing spandex any more than you would expect Philip Marlow to take up crocheting. Still, they're both going to solve the crime in the end.

Stephanie Plum has a wise attitude and prowls the streets of New Jersey. Lt. Joe Leaphorn roams the Navaho reservation using his quiet powers of observation. Again, both will find a way to get the bad guy by the end of the book.

However, over the years these characters have undergone some subtle changes: Stephanie is battling between Ranger and Morelli, while Leaphorn has lost his wife and is struggling to deal with his retirement from the Navaho Tribal Police.

Mystery characters can present a delightful dilemma with their various foibles and quirks. Kojak had his lollipop and Monk has all his particular peculiarities such as his fear of germs.

Keeping series characters fresh can be part of the battle for an author. Even in a series book, the character must grow over the course of the plot. Perhaps it is something like dealing with a sick relative. John Sandford's popular detective Lucas Davenport has gone from being a ladies' man to a family man through the course of several books.

Even in mystery/action movies, characters grow and change. Martin Riggs (played by Mel Gibson) in the *Lethal Weapon* series went from a suicide candidate to a happily married family man.

Remember these characters?
- Sherlock Holmes by Sir Arthur Conan Doyle
- Hercule Poirot by Agatha Christie
- Mike Hammer in the Micky Spillane series
- Kinsey Millhone by Sue Grafton
- Alex Cross from the James Patterson books
- Sam Spade by Dashiell Hammett
- Scully and Mulder in *The X Files* by Chris Carter
- Phillip Marlow by Raymond Chandler

Mystery

Change your heroine to fit this genre:

Mystery

Change your hero to fit this genre:

Mystery

Change your villain to fit this genre:

When you put your character in a chick-lit story be sure to consider:

(the following character elements are taken from Renee Zellweger in *Bridget Jones's Diary*)

Physical Description
- Slightly overweight but obsessed about it

Profession or Occupation
- Publishing

History
- Alcoholic binges, smoking, and can't control her weight

Relationships
- Looking for the perfect relationship

Personality
- Post-feminist

Body Language and Speech
- Sassy

Wardrobe and Possessions
- Pre-owned furniture

Environment and Daily Living
- London

Character Diamond
- CRUSADE
  - She wants to improve herself

- CAUSE
  - Because she wants love

- COMPLICATION
  - But falls for the wrong man

- CHANGE
  - She accepts herself

Chick-lit Stories

The chick-lit genre has taken off in the past few years, fueled by the popularity of such books and movies as *Bridget Jones's Diary* and the popular television series *Sex and the City*. It has brought back the use of first-person storytelling. The women in these books and movies are in many ways similar to the old first-person detectives of the past — they come armed with plenty of attitude.

Giving these characters families or mothers who always think they know best, or a circle of friends to meet for drinks, can show who that character really is. Giving the character individual quirks, fears, and vulnerabilities beyond the next shoe sale or whether she has a date for her sister's wedding can go a long way toward demonstrating this character is worth knowing.

Bridget Jones might drink too much and be overweight, but like other young women her age she is looking for love and stumbling into lots of predicaments as she tries to find it.

Carrie Bradshaw of *Sex and the City* might be successful as a columnist and author, but she can't afford to buy a condo on her own and she can't get the man she loves to shed his fear of commitment until she goes off without him. Samantha Jones comes to realize there is more to life than sex and her body when she has to deal with breast cancer and finds that the man she picked up for a one-night stand is not going away.

These are women with problems and predicaments the reader can respond to. Unlike romances where there has to be a happy ending, the chick-lit genre stands pretty much on its own. The female characters don't need to have their man at the end. They might have simply learned an important life lesson, or solved a crisis in both their love life and their job. A character might decide at the end that the two men she dates are both wrong and ends up going off on her own.

Chick-lit is no longer simply for the young, frivolous reader either. The genre has spread out and now includes its own set of subgenres, such as Mommy-lit, hilarious stories of mothers who suffer through their own set of misadventures, or Hen-lit, the stories of older women who are either trying to recapture their lost youth or going out on their own for the first time in their lives.

The important thing to remember when writing chick-lit characters is to give them life and let them have fun, but don't be afraid to make them very human inside. Put a real brain and feelings behind that sarcastic tongue.

Remember these characters?

- Becky Bloomwood from Sophie Kinsella's *Shopaholic*
- Carrie Bradshaw in *Sex and the City*
- Helen in *Raising Helen*
- Alice Chambers in *To Have and To Hold* by Jane Green
- Elle Woods in *Legally Blonde*
- Andrea Sach in *The Devil Wears Prada* by Lauren Weisberger
- Janey Wilcox in *Trading Up* by Candace Bushnell
- Joan Wilder in *Romancing the Stone*

Chick-lit

Change your heroine to fit this genre:

Chick-lit

Change your hero to fit this genre:

Chick-lit

Change your villain to fit this genre:

FINAL THOUGHTS

From Sue Viders

For my characters to be truly memorable, they have to be both heroic and flawed. Heroic in the sense she or he will go beyond the ordinary and strive for the extraordinary whether it is a physical demand, an intellectual challenge, or overcoming an emotional problem.

I like my characters flawed with some problem in their personality they have to deal with. In the story I am now writing, my heroine is dyslexic, and has a terrible time with numbers. This means of course, that if she is to continue running her small art gallery (after her partner is murdered) she will be unable to do the books, write the checks, etc. Therefore, somehow she will have to come up with a practical solution to this problem.

For me, in a romance, or a romantic suspense, the heroine also needs to be, while not necessarily beautiful, aware of herself as a woman and independent or in other words, be able to make decisions, good or bad, by herself.

Part of the trouble I have in writing, is that I am impatient to get on with the story and don't take the time to really get to know my characters. For example, my hero, in the above story, Nick, who I really love, is a strong man, but I didn't take the time to fully create him so when I got to the first meeting between the hero and heroine, I literally had no idea how he would act. And therefore I couldn't write anything.

What saved my butt was my critique group, consisting of the other three writers who helped write this book. Through our weekly breakfast meetings we have been able to work through not only my problems but everyone's character problems.

Our philosophy is we try to imagine that whatever we are reading it is our words down on the paper and therefore we try to make it the very best we can. We send our pages, limit ten pages, double spaced, via e-mail to everyone in the group by Sunday night. This gives us two days to read, edit, and think about the work. We all use the various editing systems that are already on our computers.

I work in Word, so I click on "Tools." When the menu drops down, I click on "Track Changes." Then click "Highlight Changes." And finally when that box drops down, check the box for "Track changes while editing."

This allows you, when editing, to record all the changes in red, which by the way is the best color to work in, I've tried them all, and red shows up the best. In fact, one of my critique partners calls my editing, pages full of red blood.

Sue's words of wisdom:

- Take the time to really get to know your character. Fill out all the forms in this book even if you only put down a word or two on each page.

- Find a critique group or start one yourself. But do remember, not all critique groups work. It takes time, and you may go through many different groups before one can find exactly the right mix of personalities that work together.

- In our critique group, we each have our weaknesses and our strengths. In other words, we complement each other and together, we four are one hell of a writer!

- Finally, if at all possible, physically meet, eyeball to eyeball. There is something quite wonderful that happens when you get four creative people together to brainstorm ideas and solutions. We never fail to find the answers. And you cannot do this via e-mail. There is a certain synergy that only happens when everyone talks at once and ideas flow freely back and forth.

FINAL THOUGHTS

From Lucynda Story

Often there is a question rather like the old "Which came first, the chicken or the egg?" that writers are asked. Which came first, the characters or the idea?

A lot of ideas and characters sprout from news articles and dreams. Sometimes a phrase from a song or even the song's title will provide the impetus I need to start a story.

Ninety percent of the time, I get the flash of an idea first. That spark that comes with the question, "What if...?" For me, "What if" is usually followed by this question: "Who could...?"

Ideas are all around us. A lot of mine come from current events. Having techno-geeks in the house, I'm exposed to a lot of forward thinking which inevitably ends up with one or both of those questions. Then I ask myself, "What kind of person could...?"

You'll notice the questions are open-ended. It gives me a chance to think in generalities. What type of character could work the question into an idea with potential fruit? From there I think about the character and his or her strengths and weaknesses. Once I know those, I begin the hunt for their names and try to select one that has a similar characteristic as one of my heroes, or a quality that the heroine needs to cultivate.

With their name, strengths, and weaknesses, I develop their personal backgrounds. Then I throw them into a situation, usually dealing with one of the early questions that got me thinking about developing characters to begin with and voila, I'm off to the writing races.

Since I write romances, I have a general idea of how the story will end (with a "happily ever after"). Frequently, I have a more specific ending climax in mind.

Using a plot grid and what I know about my character's backgrounds and points of conflict, I will often work from the end backward to the beginning to develop the major points of the plot.

Major points that I consider in my plots are: 1) the day that is different, 2) an unexpected change of plans, 3) the point of no return, 4) the disaster of the "black moment," and 5) the final resolution where loose ends are tied up. Once I have the major events decided, I begin writing, starting at the beginning.

Lucynda's words of wisdom:

- I use names to reveal something to me about the character.

- I get ideas from music and the news.

- I know what the final climatic scene will be.

- I take time to fill my creative mind by reading, watching movies, going for walks, taking trips, and talking with my colleagues.

Cher's words of wisdom:

- Tell your story from your heart, then go back and polish and edit.

- Go to conferences, attend workshops, and sign up for editor and agent appointments. Don't be afraid of these people. They are very nice and they love writers! They eat and sleep and have families and personal problems just like the rest of us. Not only that, editors want to buy good books and agents want to represent clients who write good books. So it's a win-win for everybody! And it's all part of networking which is vitally important to any writer.

- Voice is everything. Guard it like a rare, precious jewel and don't let *anyone* change your voice.

- If possible join a critique group or start one of your own. Leave the group if it isn't working for you because jealousy, sarcasm, and harsh comments have no place in a critique group. Staying will erode your confidence and creativity and that's the last thing any writer needs. My critique partners are invaluable to me. They are my rock and my cheering section.

- Don't be afraid to send your work out to an editor or agent.

- Lastly, I want to say a word about contests. They are great for writers in that you can receive some wonderful and helpful feedback, however, the exact opposite can happen as well. Take the judges' comments with a grain of salt. And remember that the buck stops at the editor's desk.

FINAL THOUGHTS

From Cher Gorman

Writing a book takes perseverance and a lot of mind bending, hard work. Once your brilliant tome is finished you must find the courage to send your story out to an editor or agent if you hope to get published. When your manuscript comes back to you so fast it sets your mailbox on fire, you experience the first cold sting of rejection, which can stomp your fragile writer's ego into little bits and leave a bitter taste in your mouth.

For me, it took eighteen years and so many rejections I could paper not only my walls but my neighbor's walls as well. So how did I keep going after knocking on New York's locked doors for so many years and never having them open?

To be perfectly honest, I almost gave up. In fact, right before Loose Id offered me a contract for *Wolf Island*, I had decided to keep writing but stop submitting altogether and focus my energy on learning graphic design.

However, my critique partners and fellow authors of this book, urged me — no that isn't quite right—they insisted I try submitting to a few electronic publishers before I hung up my keyboard. And I'm so glad I did. I received the contract for *Wolf Island* on April 20th and two weeks later I received another contract for *The Secret Truth at Dare Ranch* from Wings e-Press. Now it's December and this time I share a publishing contract for this character book with my critique partners. My head is still spinning.

So, where do I start when I begin work on a new project? Sometimes I discover an interesting internal conflict I want to explore. From there I begin to think about a character and a situation that might help me investigate that conflict. I have also gotten ideas from eavesdropping on conversations in the checkout line at the grocery store or from a line of dialogue in a movie or even from something my husband said to me in conversation. But I've also had characters step out of the ether into a full-blown scene in my head without knowing anything about them or the story's direction.

After the idea comes to me I go through the steps in this book — not necessarily in any particular order — to create the best three-dimensional, leap-from-the-page characters that I can. Then it's time to plot the book by making a list of scenes for each chapter and the events — external and internal — that take place in these scenes. I make sure I illustrate how each character overcomes their complications and how they change and grow into better people to deserve their happy ending by the end of the book.

Then the fun begins, it's time to start writing.

FINAL THOUGHTS

From Becky Martinez

Sometimes ideas for my books come from characters, sometimes they come from a plot idea. One thing I have learned over the years is that my story goes nowhere until my characters are set to go. If I don't know who my characters are, my plot doesn't get very far. I'm not talking about name, age, and looks. I have to know them like I know my best friend or sister or brother.

Sometimes I let them dance around in my head, trying to see what kind of trouble they can get into, how they play off each other. As they take form, I begin to check off what they look like, how they got the way they are and where they want to go. I think about motivation, fears, needs, and triumphs, until the character fully belong to me.

When I sit down to write, I need to know what these characters will do whenever I throw them a plot change, because I seldom plot much in advance.

I have a beginning and an end and a few little miseries that I cook up to drive my characters crazy, but then I let the characters guide me the rest of the way.

Over the years I've come to believe in fully rounding out not only my main characters but also some of the secondary characters who people my stories. I like to give my characters quirks or habits which show their real personality so that they become almost as vivid in my imagination as the hero, heroine, and villain. Making them more realistic makes the story more real, and hopefully helps the reader enjoy it more. Much of this background information does not appear in the book, but simply makes me understand the characters better.

As I build the back-story for all of my characters I will often write scenes that do not make it into the main story, either. It's all part of getting to know my characters. Earlier in the book we introduced the relationship chart and discussed the importance of defining moments. I will often go ahead and write up scenes that show why a relationship developed or ended as it did. The same goes for defining moments. By writing these moments down, I discover how a character felt as the event happened and I can use that as part of their memory later. I usually keep the material in a separate file that I can re-read or check later if I have questions or if I want to add something to it.

To me, if my character is fully developed, the plot will usually take care of itself. I can play with the situations or change them or use them to help my characters grow. If the character is only a shell of a person, then no matter how dynamic the plot might be, I feel the novel is incomplete.

One of my pet peeves is reading a book where the author takes great time to make certain to name all the right weapons or outline proper medical procedures, but the character is so shallow and undefined, I lose interest in the story line.

Becky's words of wisdom:

- My characters drive the plot. A fully developed character helps to get the reader involved. A fast-moving plot without a real character the reader cares about might be enjoyable at first, but if readers can't get involved with the character's needs and goals, they're not going to care what happens to that character or how the plot turns out.

- Just as you might do research on a time in history or proper police procedures, do research on who your character is and why he or she is that way. Spend some extra time getting to know the various characters in your books.

- Don't be afraid to experiment with your characters. As you get to know them you might find that they have a lot of different foibles you didn't even know about. Challenge them, question them, and make them your own.

SUMMARY

Well, all that's left are the forms as we have nothing left to tell you. We hope that as you do the various exercises and use the worksheets, your character, in either your book or movie will become more memorable and your plot stronger.

The key, or the secret, as they like to say, is to learn every possible thing you can about the fictitious people you are going to be living with over the next year or two.

Once you really know these characters, you can impart as much as you want to your audience. Making them come alive in your mind will help you to write them down on the page as flesh and blood people and not simply wooden or two-dimensional figures.

Don't be afraid to experiment. If your character didn't work as a female, make her a male or even a child or better yet — ta da, the villain.

Take time BEFORE you start writing, to really get to know your characters. In the long run, you will save time and your writing will flow more easily.

By going through the steps in this book you are well on your way to creating memorable characters. Only one more ingredient is necessary — you!

Lucynda has been quoted as saying:

"You can't get published if you don't submit.
You can't submit if you don't polish.
You can't polish if you haven't finished
and
You can't finish if you don't start."

Every project begins by taking the characters you've created and putting their story onto the page, one word at a time.

In the words of Commander Peter Quincy Taggart in *Galaxy Quest*, "Never give up, never surrender."

Your story is your dream. Go for it!

Our final, final thoughts:

Well, you've made it to the end. Hopefully you have some of your characters well developed and you are ready to start writing.

We all wish you well and hope that whatever you write will be a best seller or an award-winning movie.

Look for our classes on the Internet or at the various writing conferences in the coming years.

APPENDIX

OVERVIEW

Leftovers.

That's what we call those wonderful pages, charts, and lists we have designed and know that you will want to use, but we didn't know where to put them. So we have placed them in this appendix.

The charts on family and friends will be especially useful. We suggest you might even want to make photocopies and put them in each research notebook you have for each one of your stories.

This section includes:

- a chart for your main character's family
- a chart for your main character's friends and possibly enemies
- a "Cast of Characters" chart for the main characters in our story
- a "Cast of Characters" for your story
- a checklist of professions and occupations

Although we have not listed any research pages, since people work in different genres, it is a good idea to keep track of the various Web sites you use with notes on exactly what information you find where. You never know when, six months or even two years later, you might desperately need this information once more.

This workbook is for you to use as you see fit.

So even though we have suggested ideas and exercises for you to try, and given you charts and lists, ultimately, it is up to you to find your own style of writing.

Always remember there is no right way or wrong way...

there is only YOUR way!

WORKSHEET

Family

Character:_____

Each relative who influences the character needs:
- a full name
- how they are related
- a place and date of birth/death (if needed)
- an occupation and/or business

Consider how your character thinks or feels about this relative. Possible issues are what the character:
- likes best or least about that person
- wants to change
- wishes never happened

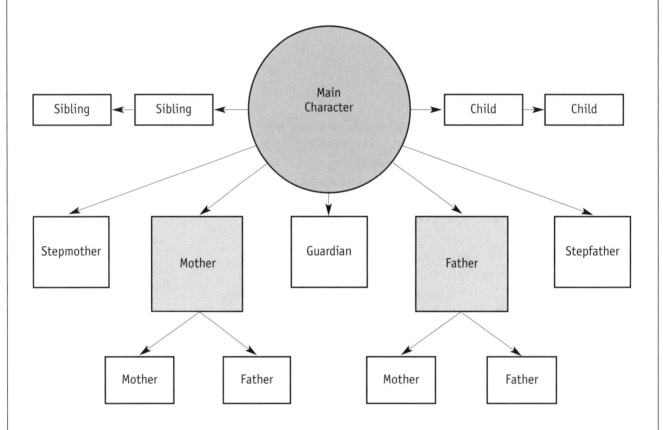

Almost Family

This might include a family housekeeper, secretary, a nanny or nurse, or someone who lives in the household and is not only close to your character but someone your character truly loves and admires.

Extended Family

This might include step-siblings, cousins, and great-aunts and uncles. You can also include/list those in the family tree who are not direct blood relations, but have married into the family and have influenced your character.

NOTE: It isn't necessary to have all of the above information for your main character. It is only needed for those family members who will in some way influence this character.

WORKSHEET

Friends

Each friend needs:
- a full name
- place and date of birth (if important)
- occupation
- and information on how they met, when, where, how, and how long they have been friends

Determine how your character feels about each friend. Possible issues include:
- why this person is their friend/enemy
- what your character derives from this friendship
- determining the binding element that keeps them friends

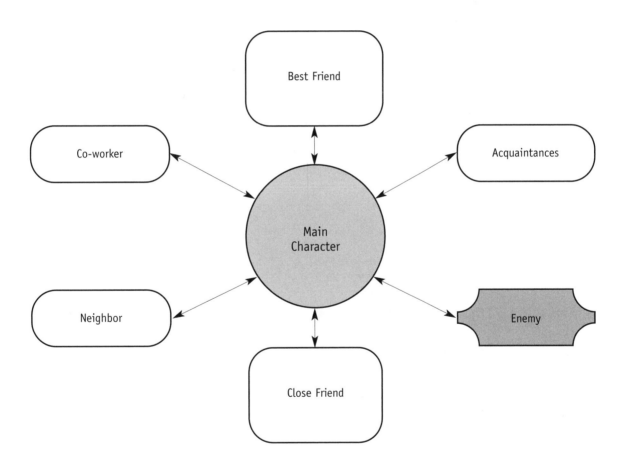

NOTE: It isn't necessary to have all of the above information. It is only needed for those who will in some way influence your characer or are needed to further the plot.

CAST OF CHARACTERS

Name	Purpose	Role	Relationship

MAIN CHARACTERS

Name	Purpose	Role	Relationship
KAYLA Turner	Prove herself innocent of killing her husband	*Heroine*	Accused of the murder of her husband Love interest to Quinn
QUINN Salazar	Find the killer	*Hero*	Investigator and Kayla's love interest
EMILY Minton	The killer	*Villainess*	Antagonist to Quinn and Kayla's relationship

SECONDARY CHARACTERS AND ANIMALS

NOTE: While all of these characters have not been mentioned before, it is necessary to know their names and the role they will play in the story.

Name	Purpose	Role	Relationship
Hector	Reflects what Quinn is missing in his life	*Confidant*	Quinn's partner
Wade Chester	Pressures on Emily	*Troublemaker*	Emily's Medical Director of the hospital
Zack	To show Kayla's caring nurturing side	*Pet*	Kayla's puppy

OFF-STAGE CHARACTERS

NOTE: These characters are referred to but never seen.

Name	Purpose	Role	Relationship
Miss Johnson	Inspiration for Emily	*Mentor*	Emily's professor
Agnes Salazar	Root of Quinn's relationship fears	*Hindrance*	Quinn's mother
Frank Salazar	Also the cause of Quinn's relationship problems	*Obstacle*	Quinn's father

WALK-ON CHARACTERS

NOTE: Needed in certain scenes to move the action along, but names are not necessary.

Taxicab driver	**Police Officer**	**Neighbor**	**Coroner**
Waitress	**Sales Clerk**	**Nurse**	**Motel owner**

CAST OF CHARACTERS

Name	Purpose	Role	Relationship

MAIN CHARACTERS

SECONDARY CHARACTERS AND ANIMALS

NOTE: While all of these characters have not been mentioned before, it is necessary to know their names and the role they will play in the story.

OFF-STAGE CHARACTERS

NOTE: These characters are referred to but never seen.

WALK-ON CHARACTERS

NOTE: Needed in certain scenes to move the action along, but names are not necessary.

CHECKLIST OF PROFESSIONS AND OCCUPATIONS

A   actor, artist, architect, advertising executive, air traffic controller, accountant, astrologist, astronaut, attorney, aerobic instructor, adult education teacher, archeologist, audiologist, acupuncturist

B   bank president, basketball star, barber, baker, bounty hunter, body guard, bomb specialist, bus driver, bank teller, beautician, bush pilot, bus boy, bartender, boxer

C   cowboy, cop, chauffeur, counselor, civil engineer, café piano player, chef, cab driver, cosmetologist, cashier, chemist, computer analyst (programmer, or hacker), cancer specialist, CEO, criminologist, call girl, captain, caterer, cattle baron, civil service employee, cartographer

D   dentist, doctor, detective, dancer, disc jockey, dental hygienist, district attorney, deep-sea diver, driver, doorman, dog handler

E   engineer, economist, emergency doctor, entrepreneur, editor, environmental activist, embalmer, explorer

F   football quarterback, factory worker, fishing guide, fire fighter, fashion designer, florist, file clerk, FBI agent, flight attendant, film editor, foley artist

G   general, gang leader, gardener, governess, gun fighter, gambler, golf pro, gymnast, geologist

H   hotel manager, human resource manager, homemaker, horse trainer, herbalist

I   investigative journalist, IRS agent, interior decorator, insurance salesman, ice skater

J   janitor, jewel thief, jockey, judge, junior executive, journalist, jailer

K   kindergarten teacher, king, kids camp counselor, karate instructor

L   loan officer, legal-aid lawyer, librarian, life guard, life coach, lecturer

M   movie director, musician, mercenary, math teacher, musketeer, missionary, mayor, maid, model, motorcycle mechanic, masseuse, magician, mime, marine biologist, mail carrier, mortician

N   newspaper reporter or editor, Navy seal, nurse, nanny, nun, nursery school owner, newscaster, nobleman, narcotics officer, night watchman

O   oil tycoon, optometrist, outlaw, oceanographer, oncologist

P   prince, pilot, police captain, principal, photographer, politician, public relations specialist, priest, pharmacist, publisher, president, psychologist, pirate, physical therapist, pet shop owner, professor, pediatric doctor, paramedic, park ranger, personal assistant, pilates instructor, princess

Q   queen, quality control agent

R   real estate agent, race car driver, receptionist, rancher, retail store buyer, revolutionary, research scientist, reporter, rabbi, restaurant owner

S   sheriff, stockbroker, soldier, small business owner, singer, scientist, safari guide, surgeon, spy, stripper, smoke jumper, sales person, Supreme Court justice, social worker, show girl, scholar, swimmer, stylist, supervisor, secretary, ski instructor, short-order cook

T   teacher, therapist, tennis player, travel writer, travel agent, talk-show radio host

U   undercover cop, union organizer, urologist, ultrasound tech

V   veterinarian, vigilante, vicar, vineyard owner, viscount

W   writer, wine merchant, waiter, welder, white water rapids guide

X   x-ray technician, x-rated movie actor

Y   yacht captain, yoga instructor

Z   zoo keeper, zoologist

NOTE: These are just a few professions and occupations that are available in today's society. Remember in historical times the choice of work was determined by ethnic issues and social standing. And this doesn't include those jobs that the writer might create in other worlds, in the future, or in other cultures.